THE PILLARS OF MY TOWN

Ken G. Gordon

Copyright © Ken G. Gordon 2024
Trinidad and Tobago, W.I.
Email: kengee3913@gmail.com
Phone: 1868 352 0491

All rights reserved. No part of this publication may be reproduced, stored in a retrieval system, or transmitted, in any form or by any means (electronic or mechanical, by photocopying, recording or otherwise), without prior permission in writing from the author/publisher except for the use of brief quotations in a book review or scholarly journal.

First Printing: 2024

Photography
Ken G. Gordon
Trinidad and Tobago, W.I.
Email: kengee3913@gmail.com

Published by
Eutille Duncan Publishing
#8-Wheeler Drive, Plymouth Road, Tobago,
Trinidad and Tobago, W.I.
Email: eutilleduncanpublishing@gmail.com
Telephone: 868-393-6725 or 868-481-4155
www.eutilleduncanpublishing.com

Produced in the Republic of Trinidad and Tobago.

"You are the light of the world. A town built on a hill cannot be hidden. ¹⁵ Neither do people light a lamp and put it under a bowl. Instead, they put it on its stand, and it gives light to everyone in the house.

In the same way, let your light shine before others, that they may see your good deeds and glorify your Father in heaven.

Matthew 5:14-16 KJV

Acknowledgements

I acknowledge Lincoln Bobb, Linton Williams, Rebecca Roberts, Lucille Percy and Jaiye Melville, son of Desmond Melville. I would also like to acknowledge Ebenezer "Cuz" George for his contributions.

I must give thanks to George Rupert Franklyn for his collaboration in putting the football club segment of my book together, a heartfelt Thank You Sir, from each and every one of us the Somerset Football Club members alive or passed on. I most definitely could not have done this without your help.

Special thanks to Mr. Winston "Man Baby" Skeete for giving me most of the information about the Goat Racing franchise.

Introduction

It is a widely known adage that a village's responsibility is to bring up its children. Well, I will attempt to do my best to go back in time, down memory lane to recall as much as I can about the heroes of my village who made my childhood growing up in Canaan/ Bon Accord /Crown Point worthwhile (I may have a few villains too). And in doing so attempt to show how my village rose to its present prominence

I laid out certain standards I lived by in my first book; *The Shadow of Fear and Hunger* and it's no doubt that my dad was integral in laying the foundation of my early life. I was fortunate to have had him in my life for almost the first eighteen years, he died quite early. And even though those years were not very pretty, the positive seeds he sowed were never neglected.

Having said that, I must let every one of my readers know that whenever I refer to **"my village"**, from here on, I mean Canaan/ Bon Accord/ Crown Point.

The entrepreneurs of my village were my heroes, and they were many. I intend to show how my village became the town it has developed into today, because of those entrepreneurs. I aim to show that these men and women were just magnificent in their fields and anyone worth his weight in common sense paid attention if he wanted to make something of his life, and I did, I really noticed. We learn from those who went before us. From their examples we choose our own path. I will also highlight those who had the biggest impact on my life growing up.

Beginning with the acquisition of Kilgwyn's Coconut Estate, which was on the left side of Canaan, (I'm not aware of who had the foresight to do so). Coming into Canaan, from Scarborough, our village was mainly on the right side of the main road facing the estate going to the airport, and Bon Accord mainly on the left side of the road. The Bon Accord Coconut estate also had a similar transition and opened more space for developments. There was Friendship Estate also, but of the four coconut estates only Mr. Frank Latour's estate still thrives in coconuts.

There was a Shirvan Park Racetrack (for horse racing) which was a part of Mr. Latour's property. Now, that too has become a developed area with stores and businesses including a Pharmacy (which stays open to 7.00 pm at night), Digicel and MoneyGram offices, two restaurants, and even a doctors' office. The Tobago House of Assembly's Division of Food Security, Natural Resources and the Environment and the Tobago Licensing Office in the building next door are all located where that racetrack used to be.

On the side where Kilgwyn Coconut Estate used to be there's now Dave's Discount Hardware, The Tobago Technology Center, Stumpy's Emporium, The Tobago Taxi-Cab Cooperative Society building, Unique's Furniture Store, The Tobago Nutrition Cooperative Society, Ansa Car Sales, a Steelpan Tent and the first Canaan Housing Project, to name a few. The second housing project, Milford Court, is on part of where the Bon Accord estate occupied.

Regarding the Crown Point area, I believe it was always going to be the first to develop and be as lively as it has become today because it surrounds the only airport and is in close proximity to two of the most famous beaches on our island, Store Bay and Pigeon Point.

My village has all the infrastructure for a thriving young town. There are two banks; Republic Bank and First Citizens Bank. The First Citizen's bank is a modern-day facility at the beginning of Canaan, erected about a year ago, with all the latest technology of course.

First Citizens Bank was previously located on the same sight, on some sort of lease arrangement, where our first post office was situated over seven decades ago for almost ten years. Then having noticed that business and financial profits benefited them at that location, they made the decision to purchase property and erect their own new structure making Canaan a permanent business address.

There are ATMS with access to funds of the banks that are not represented by a structure. We also have Eastern Credit Union and Unit Trust. There are three huge supermarkets, a car dealership, there are five Pharmacies, an all-night gas station, government offices at D Colosseum. And several restaurants and casinos, hotels and guesthouses, to name some of the amenities.

My village is rich in every avenue one can think of, so we are not easily pushed aside for recognition. We were, and are still rich in sportsmen and women, an athletic club and two of the best football and cricket teams ever to pass through Tobago; Western Springfield Athletics, Somerset Football Club and Starlight Cricket Club. I will expound some more on these clubs' achievements as we go along.

My village boasts of some of Tobago's best tradesmen; carpenters, masons, straighteners, painters, tailors, welders, electricians, traffickers, barbers, plumbers, and shoemakers. We were and are well equipped to handle any emergency that comes our way. We also have hardware, plumbing and electrical shops located throughout the village. If you name it or just think you have need of it, Canaan can supply it.

I am most interested in the commercial field where we as a town excel. The business community grew up steadfast and strong. If you look around today you can clearly see the evidence on every block or corner you pass. I am so impressed by what I see that it makes me walk with my head held high everywhere I go. I have so much pride in my stride because it feels wonderful to be known as being from Canaan.

We have the input of great teachers, starting with our pre-school teacher Annetta "Baby Joe" Archer, I never knew her first name until recently. My first chance at learning came in her nursery school at Canaan's lodge. I can boast that she was instrumental in putting out teachers, assemblymen, doctors, nurses, lawyers and even a police commissioner, just to list a few of her accomplishments, and of course your humble servant writing these words here right now.

Although I must warn you beforehand that I was not as fortunate as the rest of them who completed their full education and it was not for the want of trying. I tried my darndest, even walked seven and a quarter miles (7 1/4) to high school but was still denied my right to a full education by the principal, can you just imagine? story in my first book *("The Shadow of Fear and Hunger.")*

It seemed like the men and women of our village would just go to bed one night and decide by maybe a dream or some premonition they got during the night that they should start some type of business venture that the community would benefit from. The community rewarded them for their ideas by providing them the environment in which to do business. This made our village a better place to live.

The surrounding communities soon realized that instead of having to spend all that money going to Scarborough it was more convenient to come and do business in our village. It was closer for walking because transportation was scarce at that time.

Those business ideas helped to create the village we inherited today with some of the biggest buildings in any village in Tobago, and they are getting bigger every year. There is a four storied one, with a basement, right opposite my home; the Tobago Taxi-Cab Co-operative building.

My village was and is considered the *"breadbasket of Tobago".* We boast even more impressive buildings than Scarborough, the capital town of Tobago, from which, would you believe, there was a migration of businesses and churches to Canaan. Who did not migrate, opened branches.

I was told that at one time there was an attempt by the government to create another town, at Plymouth, through planning and special constructions. It didn't work out for Plymouth. Government intervention was not needed for my village. The residents through their own will, foresight and expertise, naturally did it without external interference.

Compared to the rest of the villages on the island, growing up here during the fifties and sixties was indeed a privilege and an education. Regardless of hurricane Flora and the few years following, because we were a resilient community, we bounced back in a way that even our sister isle Trinidad did not think possible. There were shops of all types to keep our village going, if you needed flour, rice, rum, wine and beer, curtains, bakeries or a truck for sand or gravel we had them here. We even had a concrete factory where cylinders, blocks and inverts were made.

Being able to finally fulfill my dream of putting all this together to showcase the selfless achievements of some of the past heroes and pillars of our society, really gives me more pleasure and satisfaction than I expected. There's a special feeling which comes with the past connections I had with most of these heroes, though at the time I didn't know the significance of those relationships and the impact they were leaving with me. That in 2024 I would be doing this in their honour. I am rather proud of those past associations because everyone can now see the impact they had on Tobago.

Business and

Infrastructure

Chapter One

As I happened to mention hurricane Flora in my introduction, I will say a bit more about her and her impact on my village. It was on the thirtieth day of September nineteen sixty-three around eleven that morning that she paid us a visit we will never forget. For the younger ones reading this, I remember it as though it was yesterday.

I was sixteen years old, and my dad had been in a car accident. He had just come out of hospital with a fractured foot two days before. He was walking on crutches, and could do almost nothing for himself so I had to cook for both of us. I decided on dumplings and saltfish with ochroes in coconut milk that day. And just as I took the saltfish off the stove we heard a roar coming from the back of the house on the northern side, I never tasted that dumpling and saltfish on that Monday. All I had time to do about lunch was take out my dad's food and start to brace myself for what was about to happen.

Almost everyone had a battery radio in those days, so we heard it announced to expect this woman, Flora, coming to visit, and what she could do to our homes. Before I could give my dad, his food and go inside to close all the windows, she was upon us fiercer than we could have imagined.

That wind was without any mercy coming from the north and it started by throwing down our coconut trees as if they were just corn stalks. One of those trees fell on our roof knocking off the galvanize sheets on the northwestern side of our house in the process, and the rain that came with it was on us all at once. The rain that came in when the tree fell destroyed the rest of the food. I saw an eight-foot spouting from our neighbor's roof get torn off and it flew and hugged a coconut tree trunk as if it had been nailed there by a carpenter, just to show the strength of that wind.

That portion of our roof that was blown off exposed us to the unwanted rain and our clothes were soaked through in no time flat. My dad, being in no condition to do anything, just sat in a chair like a wounded rat, soaked to the bone. Looking at him I felt pity, even though he was such a *"bad man",* all the badness was washed out of him that day. Anyway, the wind and rain continued from the north for about another half hour then it passed over us and went to the south. Then we heard it coming back with a vengeance, as if to say; *"if you thought I was finished with you all, you are mistaken"*.

Our front door faces the south, and it came through that door with such force that my brother (who was trying to get to his home) and I, were putting both our shoulders behind that door and we could not keep that wind out. Just imagine this, my brother was always overweight he was around five feet eight inches and about two hundred and fifty pounds, and I was about five feet six inches with a stockily built frame weighing around one hundred and seventy pounds, but both of us still could not keep that wind out. It just blew open the door like if it had bought our house so we had no say anymore. Whatever she wanted to do, she just did. The house was in disarray, everything blown everywhere to its pleasure, and there was not one thing we could do about it.

Flora died down about an hour later and everyone went outside, except my dad, to see the extent of the destruction.

The roads were blocked, trees were everywhere across the road, nothing could pass. Our home was ruined, everything was all over the place and wet.

We had a small parlor where I used to sell snow-cones, cakes and soft drinks, it was made by noggin built with our own hands from money my dad had won at the racetrack. To my surprise it was untouched by the hurricane. I put my dad on my back to take him into that parlor. I managed to do it, I think with the help of God, because at sixteen I really didn't know how I did it, but I got him there. And that's where we lived out the months until we repaired our roof.

In the months that followed Flora, help came into the island from all the other countries of the Caribbean and Central America. We had corned beef and cheese and other tinned meats I had never seen before; the only thing was standing in line for hours to get it. It reminded me of the earlier years not long after the Second World War when I had to do the same thing with a ration card in my hand to receive supplies at Steward's Shop in Canaan.

Eventually, after some months, we got a supply of material for our roof, and had it repaired, and we moved back into our home.

Chapter Two

As highlighted in my introduction my village quickly recovered from Flora mainly because of our collective resilience and our wide range of entrepreneurs.

So, I would like to start in the Crown Point area and recognize and mention Mr. Bertie Crooks, truck owner, for all the sand and any other home construction materials one might need. In those times a truck driver could just choose a beach to back his truck onto and have his loaders fill it with sand, free of charge, while gravel came from the Goldsborough River for a small fee.

Mr. Crooks was also interested in community enhancement because he came up with the idea, that would benefit our entire village and surrounding areas; of introducing a successful garbage collection routine for the whole community. He was also available to go to the port to transport foodstuffs from the ferry, which came from Trinidad, to the shops all over Tobago. He was a busy man.

He was also the owner of horses. One special one called *"My Own",* won quite a few races at Shirvan Park. We had our own horse racing track at Shirvan up until 1984, when it was destroyed by fire. As I mentioned in the introduction it was owned by the Latours; owners of the only coconut estate still left in existence, of the four in this area.

Mr. Crooks was also reputed for buying up lands around the airport and was responsible for being the man who started the development of the area.

Then there were some rumors/speculations that my great uncle Alphonso Philbert Theophilus "Fargo" James bought some land around the airport area too. But because of the lack of governmental administration and lack of the proper paperwork for administrative purposes for ownership, Fargo died without rightful ownership of said properties being acknowledged.

Even today there are still properties in Tobago that are without legal documentation because of the same lack of proper administration services rendered by our government headquarters based in Trinidad. But they can acquire properties from three and four generations of families for below market value for a runway extension at Gaskin while the whole community still must hear water trucks passing day and night to supply the village hotels with water.

We who live here in this part of the village must contend with no water in our taps, without any warnings, even worse than in the old days when Water and Sewerage Authority (WASA) would send around a truck ringing a bell so customers could know there would be no water in their taps. In this modern era, we have to contend with our taps just yawning on us when we open them. And that happens on a regular basis every week. While I am writing this there's no water in my taps here at my home, and it's been gone since 9.07am this morning and it's now after 11.00 pm. I had to use bottles of water to bathe.

I ask this question of our educated authorities: *"Where will the extra visitors get water for basic use when that runway is completed, and they check into their hotels?"* The idea of the runway and airport extension is to facilitate more comfortable movement of visitors. They would need water too; didn't our educated pawns/puppets take some time to think about that?

I got carried away a bit, I guess, but just a few weeks ago a one hundred-million-dollar WASA project was initiated from Lambeau down to Friendship in Canaan, to stop all our water woes in my community and up to yesterday my taps were dry. I am just asking where did the water go? Or did all of that money really go into that specific project? Or like Donald Trump would say, *"fake news".* It really makes one wonder, ent? That's why I always ask for a deduction in my water rate payment for the days I do not receive water. I think that I should not have to pay for what I did not receive.

Long ago when I went to the shop to buy a pound of sugar, I had the prerogative to stand where I could see the shopkeeper put the pound weight on the scale. And watch him throw the sugar in the paper bag until a pound was weighed by the scale balancing itself to tell me loud and clear it was a pound of sugar I was getting for my money When I go to pay for water at the WASA office, they throw this big word in my face every time I bring up the topic of not getting a steady supply of the most important commodity in one's life. The water is **SUBSIDIZED**. When I tell them I cannot drink or boil their subsidy, and I get laughed out of the office.

With all the educated intelligence the powers-that-be have, with all their university degrees and acumen they lack simple common sense, which was there long before books. They are simply just putting the proverbial cart before the horse.

Water is life! This is the year Twenty Twenty-four not the Nineteen Fifties. It is also said that *"the pen is mightier than the sword"*, so let us see if that is true. I have done my part here.

I look forward to positive results in the near future, we deserve to have water in our taps non-stop, on a daily basis without any delay. It's our basic right as citizens, we are not aliens here in Tobago. **IT'S OUR BASIC HUMAN RIGHT!**

I have in my possession an article from the Trinidad Guardian dated Friday July 12th, 1957, which says, and I

Photograph of article in the Trinidad Guardian dated Friday 12th July 1957, indicating governments promise to solve water problems throughout Trinidad and Tobago by 1960.

quote: "Trinidad Likely to Solve Water Problem By 1960" said a Mr. J.D. Atkin, a Water Biologist employed with Works and Hydraulics Department. It's what he told the South Trinidad Chamber of Commerce at their meeting on that day. I can just imagine how they all applauded that statement, but to have Mr. Atkin here today to see the ridiculousness of the water system and to hear of the kind of expenditure used up for the better state of affairs for water. And the useless, unashamed utilities minister (U. U. U.), who is a very good talker on the television with no water behind it, how does he sleep at night? He *"can fool some of the people some of the time, but he cannot fool all of the people all of the time"* like he tries to do.

We often wake up and there's no water in our taps. Taking our taxpayers money every month for false promises and pretense, he's a big shot talker who cannot handle his portfolio, a typical politician, all talk and no substance, otherwise I would not be writing this now. With so much faeces /excrement remaining in our toilets because of water not being available to flush, I would suggest that most of it be used to shoot at the Minister responsible, just for him to believe it's there to be shot, and it starts at the top.

No one can ever know how long water will be in our taps when it comes, so it's a rush to do everything concerning water when it's available. And never forget to fill up everything that can hold water.

In 2024. Another idea that can be put to work is to pay the Minister according to how we receive water. When there's no water in our taps, the Minister should not get paid, simply. Again, it starts at the top. Daily life in our town is jeopardized constantly at the thought of this crucial unreliable water system. For coming on the television and bragging about the millions spent on new water programs, as if he's doing the country a favor, no water, no pay. For treating our citizens with scant courtesy because he says they spent millions on what is our right, as long as we do not receive water, he should not be paid.

My question for the wonderful minister: "Were all those millions of proverbial eggs put in the same water basket? Because it seems like that basket broke and all those eggs went their different ways. I am using this medium to say it like I see it, by calling a spade a spade. In other words, if it looks like a duck, walks like a duck, quacks like a duck, under normal circumstances it must be a duck. If the Minister is being paid for not doing what he should be paid for, then why is he being paid? If we cannot receive water in our taps, whom should we blame? Except the Minister with the responsibility. I have said it before, this has been happening since the 1950s, enough is enough. Don't kill my new town. I reiterate, this is no joke, I really need to have water 24/7 as my God given right to take care of my family. I'm sure he, the utilities minister, doesn't have a water problem at his home where he lives, positive. Who the cap fits just draw the string tight.

People here in Tobago are just enriching the hardware stores by buying their water tanks, pumps and plumbing just to be comfortable. I think it's an unwanted high price to pay for the right to have water in our taps. It's like I have to pay twice for the same commodity. This is most definitely not right or fair to anyone who is considered a citizen of this country. This brings me to say over and over again; this is *"Trinidad **but** Tobago"*. Tobagonians are the stepchild, the bastard picknie! All the signs, habits and practices point in that direction, as God is my witness!!!

I was ten years and nine days old on that date; July 12th, 1957. My guess now is that as he didn't say Trinidad **and Tobago**, it meant that our needs were not included within his findings, why doesn't that surprise me? Because we still suffer ridiculously with water shortages where I live in Canaan, Tobago, even now, in the year 2024, which is, wait a minute my old brain depends on a calculator to count the number of years that have elapsed.

It has been sixty-six years since. And would you please believe me when I say that we still have that same water problem of the 1950s today, not being able to change that old system and deliver an adequate supply of water to my community, it's as if the years have not passed by. Maybe we are living in limbo in a land where time stood still.

It always pains me to understand why when I travel to the other Caribbean islands and stay at any hotel, big or small, I am never out of water in my room, whether day or night, and every day of the week. Even islands much smaller than Trinidad and Tobago like; Grenada, Barbados, St Lucia and St. Vincent.

I think I can remember when most of those islands came to our late prime minister Dr Eric Williams, the "Godfather" of the Caribbean, cap in hand, seeking among other things, loans for upgrading their infrastructure so they could be where they are today. Taking all our monies to invest in good hospitality.

In contrast, when tourists come to Tobago, they would check into a hotel or guesthouse with the hope of receiving the hospitality they deserve, but on doing so they find out that water is not available for even washing their hands. I should know because those water trucks keep running day and night transporting water to those hotels and guesthouses in order to keep them open.

Nothing else is left for their guests to do but to pack up and leave without paying, and no one can blame them for leaving, because the owners did not hold up their end of the agreement. This in turn becomes the owner's loss of revenue, and they still have their bills to pay.

I was reliably told that just before Covid (in 2020) the small hotels and guesthouses were loaned money for refurbishment of the buildings so that occupancy would be raised for visitors. They still adopt this attitude that quantity is more important than quality, because the water shortage never came into play, as regards increased occupancy. Maybe this was because the villagers here would get a well-earned relief from suffering all those years (the number Is sixty-six years), a full lifetime for some people. I think it's because we are such a peaceful people in Tobago, we are not tire burners and road blockers like the Trinidad protestors, we are taken for granted, but a change is going to have to come. Tobago people always say; "Wha nuh meet yuh, naah pass yuh" and "pick sense outta nonsense."

The question remains, if the smaller islands could have had the foresight to prepare from since that time, where were our powers-that-be who were in charge of that utility hiding, under which house, stool or table, or maybe they didn't go to school that day. Maybe it rained. They usually have so many university degrees behind their names, and no understanding of the simple basics. Common sense *"mek"* before book.

It really bogles my mind to experience the lack of good planning on the part of whomever oversaw water distribution at that time. The water situation as it is now might just have been able to supply the population of 1957, if one wants to speculate. Maybe they never thought that we could get to 1,400,000 (One point four million) citizens.

After all, this is not China, where it was designated at one time, that families must not have more than one child for a certain number of years. This is Trinidad and Tobago where partying and bacchanal is the population's favorite culture, what did they expect to happen after all that drinking and partying? Church services?

Sometimes in my reverie I get lost in thoughts, that Trinidadians as a whole, get jealous of us because we have done without so many essentials in our lives as Tobagonians, because we have very little to work with, and because of the fact that we can still compete with them on almost every facet of society. So, not giving us the water we need is no big thing, we should handle that as nothing, or as everything else. Well, no more, in 2024. Enough is just that, enough. The Minister is a Trinidadian.

I am of the belief that as we can do so much with so little, it scares them, because it shows them up as lazy or lacking sustainable talent. But we are just more resourceful having to do more with much less, we have become acclimatized to the simple term of getting up to get things done, no procrastination.

We gave the country a President, a Governor of the Central Bank, a Chief Justice, an Attorney General, a Commissioner of Police, two Prime Ministers, a Head of the Public Service, and if you go through the rest of our country, you will find a Tobagonian in every nook and cranny of the society.

We are never the people to sit with our chin in our hands and complain to others, feeling sorry for ourselves, we get up and get. Except for the current ministers who were sent to Trinidad parliament to represent us. They were cut from a different bolt of cloth from the rest of us because as soon as they got there it's only lip service and scant courtesy, we get from both of them and those before too. I'll explain a little later on in this book exactly what I'm talking about with those who are supposed to speak for us.

Chapter Three

Let's talk about travel; in the earlies the Crown Point Airport, now known as the A.N.R. Robinson International Airport, was just a small building built and opened for business in 1940 with a 2,200-foot grass runway constructed on a foundation of rocks and gravel overlaid with turf. The runway was later lengthened in 1942 to 5,000 feet mainly for the use of American airplanes during the Second World War. Later in the 1960s it was lengthened to 6.500 feet (after hurricane Flora in 1963 the last 500 feet had to be condemned). It was again lengthened to 9,000 feet in the mid-1980s. along with the upgrades of a new terminal building, access roads and car parks.

Inside the main building of the original airport (1940-1980) there was a big scale to weigh bags, a long counter for incoming passengers to show their tickets to staff, and that most important amenity, a telephone in the corner of that long counter. In those days without that telephone airport staff could not know whether the airplane would arrive or not, it was replaced by the traffic controllers of today.

On the outside of the building there were two carts to transport the bags to and from the airplane, sometimes these carts were attached to a jeep according to the number of bags. The jeep was also used to patrol the runway before the flights landed and departed, because sometimes animals (like cows and sheep) would lie on the grass after feeding.

When my dad was employed at the airport, he drove that jeep. I would help him light the lanterns along the runway for night flights. I must say that was when my curiosity started about travelling to other countries, wanting to know where the flights came from and where they were going.

There was no tower to accommodate traffic controllers, just a phone call to inform the staff of the time-of-flight arrival/departure. And that's when we, my dad and I, would jump into the jeep and go the length of the runway to clear the animals or light the lanterns according to the times of the flights. By the way the lanterns, like the customary *bou'eille d'feu* were filled with kerosene.

There was a roundabout in front and to the left when approaching the main entrance to the building, with big almond trees within the circle, and a small car park. On the western side of the building there was the garage for the fire engine and fire officers' quarters. Also, a tractor for Mr. Ifill Dillon to cut the grass on the runway.

Above; aerial view of the old Crown Point Airport (1940-1980).

In 1987 the central government of Trinidad and Tobago invested $78.7 million TT dollars to upgrade and develop the Crown Point Airport. The project was completed in 1992 and the first wide-bodied aircraft landed on it in that same year. Since then, visitors to our island can come directly to Tobago from America and Europe.

Above front entrance of the A.N.R. Robinson International Airport at Crown Point present day. (2024). Below; runway of the A.N.R. Robinson International Airport

As an old truck driver, I would like to change gears a bit. I would like to mention that group of men who made a huge difference when they started The Tobago Taxi-Cab Cooperative Society. I think it was somewhere in the 1960s.

As far as I know they started just as an association through the tourist industry creating tours throughout the island, for the cruise ships that grace our shores every year at the beginning of the cold season in Europe and America. I saw where they moved from just Taxis to taking over the rental of Beach Facilities in certain villages. Then they bought and still own and manage a gas station at Scarborough. Then they purchased property at Canaan and constructed a four storied building, which houses several other businesses along with their head office.

I do admire the tenacity of Mr. David Antoine, Mr. Adolphus James and Mr. Herman Thomas, and all the taxi men who came together and worked their way towards achieving those goals. In that new building they have the privilege to house companies like Eastern Credit Union Co-operative Society Limited, The Unit Trust Cooperation and their Tobago Taxicab Co-operative Society head offices and many others.

The initiative of this co-operative and others like it is to seek local interests. They employ locals and give something back to the immediate community, which in the long run is what it is all about, and what better way to help your own people. These guys saw the need and just took the initiative and it all paid off in big dividends, and made the years fruitful. They are just reaping exactly what they sowed.

The foundation for that four storied building didn't start a few years ago when they poured the first load of concrete and laid the first block, it started in the 1960s when they held their first meeting as the Tobago Taxicab Cooperative society. I tip my hat to that core of gentlemen who I call visionaries. Another set of pillars to take a bow.

Above; photograph of Tobago Taxi Cab Co-operative Complex; side view.

Front view of Tobago Taxi Cab Co-operative Complex.

Chapter Four

Another of my heroes was made because of those two beaches mentioned earlier. Because of the revenue to be had from them we had several taxi men and reef boat owners as well as tour guides *"born"* right here at Crown Point.

I can recall one of my favorite heroes started as a taxi-cab driver then became a reef boat owner, then a proprietor, and owner of the renowned Golden Star Restaurant, Bar and Night Club. His name was Mr. John Grant, entrepreneur extraordinaire. I call him the cream of the crop, as he stands out prominently above many of the rest, and he is someone to measure oneself by.

He started off as a taxi-cab driver and used all his resources to maintain the status he wanted for himself and just elevated his life to be the best example he could set for younger ones like me. Being the shrewd businessman, he also bought several properties throughout the island and being the father of one child who lived in Canada, he just fulfilled his dream and went forward to be the best he could be.

If you wanted to have international entertainment John Grant's Golden Star was the place to be for a weekend, and the Tobago leg of Scouting for Talent was held at Golden Star. The winner represented Tobago at the finals in Trinidad.

I distinctly remember dancing to the late Mr. Eddie Lovette, a Jamaican superstar artiste, live at John Grant's Golden

Star. John also owned the first Pancake House in Tobago, it was situated at the corner of John Gorman Street and Milford Road, Bon Accord. But all good things must come to an end sometime, and with the years comes the time to call it quits. From the years of plenty came the time for him to retire and with no relative to rely on to carry on his legacy he began to liquidate his assets, which by now were in the millions.

As testimony to my admiration of this man, presently there is a multi-million-dollar building being erected on that same property of Golden Star that Grant sold before he retired, right now if you drive down to Crown Point and look across from D Colosseum, another massive investment owned by another Tobagonian entrepreneur named Spence, you will

Above; location of the former John Grant's Golden Star restaurant, bar and nightclub. Currently site of new construction.

see the construction in progress. The foundation of which was set there by none other than that self-made, driven, taxi-cab driver. It also reminds me of a saying: *"He came, He saw, He conquered."*

I can remember visiting John at his home, he was in his eighties and there was a contingent of outstretched hands all seeking that pound of flesh. Each man for himself, looking for that hand-out to make their ends meet, I watched, and I learned well. I don't think his retirement went well, not having any well-meaning relatives around him. I noticed too it's one thing to be successful in business in one's youth but if you don't put things in place for retirement the predators start circling in droves. It reminds me of that big ugly black bird that circles at Sea Lots at that dumping ground, the corbeau/vulture. One might say there are none in Tobago, you will be mistaken, they are here in human form, friends beware.

He ended up in a home for the aged, he had the money for that, but the care was not that of the love and understanding you get from a close relative. And because of it I would see him almost every day in a taxi of his choice going to purchase his lunch at different restaurants according to his taste buds on that day. It pains me to relate this part of my story because I always say that those homes are not for retired people who have sons or daughters, because fathers and mothers tend to live much longer with that special child's care, with their love being returned.

In memoriam, I must say I will always treasure the memory of Mr. John Grant and all that he did for himself and by extension this community. I appreciated being around him, learning all the while. his legacy will forever be in my memory and I will cherish the selfless contributions he made to enhance our community. He was a beacon of hope for those of us who take the time to learn from those, like him, who left their mark for us to hold on to. Thank you, John, for sharing those valuable times with me. May you rest in eternal peace shaded under the wings of love, having left your footprints here on our sands of time, for whomever to see and gratefully appreciate.

Chapter Five

As I move along, I must venture way back to my first day of school at Bishop's High School, Tobago. That would have been early in the year nineteen fifty-nine. My dad bought me a new bicycle to ride to school from Canaan to Mt Marie and I was thrilled to be in the company of one of my neighbors in the person of Mr. Russell Martineau. We had as our third party to ride with us another neighbor, the young and beautiful Ms. Juanita Hunte. So, we had very stimulating conversations to accompany us every morning and afternoon. There was never a dull day and we all looked forward to our precious times together.

At that point in time, I called Russell Dan. Growing up here in Canaan that was the name everyone called him. I knew his mom as Ma Lena Martineau; owner of the best parlor in Canaan. There was where we all got our mauby and Cowie's rock cakes, when we had the money.

Dan was always a bright boy, just by listening to him anyone could tell he was intelligent, and I was happy to know that we were in the same house at school, which was Reid. The other houses were Anstey, Davies and Bowles. We would compete for house points in every aspect of our education, be it sports or examinations or deportment, those were the rules of our school. I was really surprised to find out that Dan was a sprinter just like me when our sports came around, he was fast too.

I must say that because of my school history, moving here and there, I could not follow Dan's career path. Eventually I was told he was at some university studying law. It made me very happy and proud to know that my neighbor had elevated himself to that degree academically.

Now when I look at his credentials, I have no idea what half of them mean, but I am impressed to see one of our *"little black boys"* made it to the heights he did. The knowledge that he came from a single parent home, raised by a parlor owner to where he reached, is such a credit to his character that no one can say it is impossible to be the best you can be if you put your mind to it.

When I google his name now, I see Mr. Russell Martineau S.C., CMT, LLM (Lond.), I don't have a clue what all those letters mean but I am completely impressed. Because a little further down that page I also see that he was Attorney General of Trinidad and Tobago for five years from 1981 to 1986. He was a former member of the Law Commission. He was also a tutor at the Hugh Wooding Law School and a former part-time lecturer in Commercial Law at the University of the West Indies.

He was called to the Bar of England in Wales in 1972. He was Senior Counsel since 1993 and is a member of the Bar in England, Barbados, Antigua, St. Lucia, Grenada, St. Vincent and Trinidad and Tobago. He is president of the Law Association of Trinidad and Tobago. He was chairman of the Tobago Plantations Limited.

He is Chairman of the Board of L. J. Williams Limited, Home Constructions Limited. Chairman of the A. N. R. Robinson Library Museum and Ethics Centre. Director of Guardian General Limited and Republic Financial Holdings Limited from 1999 to January 31st 2018.

He has publications in "The Lawyer" and edited the digest of cases.

This man I rode to school with can practice law in countries where I can only travel to and get a sea bath. He has so many accolades to his name that just saying them could intimidate opponents. I am proud to say that he was one of my heroes and the inspiration gained from even being associated with him gives me goosebumps at having known him from such an early age. He is another stalwart of our community and a most distinguished pillar of our society.

Coming from this small community we had another stalwart in Mr. Hilton Guy, who had a career as a policeman spanning almost 40 years and eventually became Commissioner of police in 1998 and he served for 5 years. Can you just imagine the tenor of the man, coming from our small village, joining the service to do good for the community then rising to the top of the ladder to be the man in charge? The man I knew, the confidence he had, I think I can truly say that it was all a part of his plan.

I cannot say much about the private life of the man, because after a few years, while moving up in the ranks, I think Tobago became too small to contain him. He moved to Trinidad, and eventually that move took him to the top of his profession, which I think, was well deserved and his ultimate goal. I knew his entire family and I knew how proud they were of his ambition, for all his accomplishments I say congratulations for a job well done. I can say I knew him well enough to award him this citation as a pillar of our community and that he represented himself very well throughout his life, and he has my total respect. I heard about his passing and my condolences go out to his wife Trixie and their boys.

Chapter Six

I can also remember the first gas station at Milford, owned and operated by none other than Mr. Allan "Recto" Horsford. It was the first gas station in this area and owned by a member of this village, there was a tire shop there as well. This man took up the challenge to make this community a better place than how he met it, by installing a gas station near to the airport. He knew business would be great in the area where taxis, other motor vehicles and reef boats frequented. He came up with this idea and he made it happen. Just think of the sacrifice that went into all his planning, and all because of community spirit.

I can imagine that he never knew what he started would turn out to be the foundation for what is known today as the first and only 24/7 gas station on the island of Tobago. It accommodates trucks, cars and fuel for reef boats and fishing boats. What vision for another humble villager, and another hero who cannot be forgotten for his selfless thoughtfulness.

The gas station was taken over by his son Roland after he passed on. Roland did the best he could right up to the time it exchanged hands when he neared retirement and thought it was the best for new owners to control it and take it further into the future. And they have done so, employing many people, and helping all those families.

I can also remember a little short lady called Ms. Molly Sandy, who I learnt was of the Moriah Sandys, and no relative to the Canaan Sandys, but for me a Sandy was a Sandy, "all ah we ah one family". She owned the first Drug

Store, as we called it in those days, seeing the need for medicines in Canaan.

This building housed the first drugstore in Canaan. It has been renovated and now houses a Roti shop and an Ice-cream Shop.

That small but significant venture became the nearest pharmacy for anyone in the whole western half of the island, and everyone would come for any of their medicinal needs. I think the idea was genius on her part, and kudos go out to that gentle lady for her stella contribution. All I can remember is that she had a small black car called a Prefect, I think it was a Ford. She had that Drug Store right at the corner of Milford Road and Douglas Street, Canaan. The original building still stands today, of course some refurbishing was done over time.

Today we are a town with five Pharmacies strategically placed so that everybody shares a piece of the proverbial pie. What Ms. Molly Sandy started at Douglas Street has blossomed to fruition and she must be smiling down from heaven right now and giving herself a well-deserved pat on her back. Taking all the credit for the pioneer that she turned out to be.

Chapter Seven

I am about to change gears here somewhat again; I must mention three of the best mechanics I ever had the pleasure of watching at work. They were Mr. Claude Joseph, Ewitts and his brother Arnold Douglas.

Claude was at his best with Land Rovers, although he worked on other vehicles too, but everyone would witness the joy he got from working on his favorite jeep. I can assume that this love of this type of vehicle might have come from being around so many when he was in the police service. Yeah, he was a police officer too, but I think he retired early to finish his days doing what he loved best, repairing Land Rovers at his leisure. It's like I always say; it's not work when you are doing the thing you love, it's like being paid for having fun or taking people's money under false pretenses.

I can also remember Claude doing a repair job on the engine of the first car I owned in 1973. When I bought it, I knew it needed work on the engine, but as it was in driving condition, I took the chance and bought it anyway. I started looking for the best in the field because I wanted a good job done. I contacted Ewitts and Arnold as they were my relatives, but they had eight to four jobs and it was not possible to have their services, so I went to Claude, and he took the job.

That was my first car of fifty-one cars that I bought. I had a small business in used cars, buying and repairing them one at a time. I resold around forty-nine, all for profit, one without making anything. I am now driving number fifty-one, a new one I bought, as I'm not as young as I used to be.

Any way back to the first car; Claude did a complete overhaul of the engine, he changed rings, gaskets, points, plugs, cylinders, timing belt, the works, and to the day he promised to finish the job, he was right on time. I was ready to try out my new engine because that's what I got from Claude, a new engine.

I even took him with me for a test drive, and he explained how I should break in that new engine. In my excitement I even forgot to pay him until after the test drive, I had to apologize to him because I knew what I was paying for was the best, I didn't have to drive it to be convinced. He just smiled knowing it was my first car he understood it was because of the excitement.

That was Claude at his best, after all he went to Bon Accord primary school same as me, with the same motto; *"good work or none"*. It showed in his character; in the satisfaction he got delivering a well-done job to his client. And his good name continues to be spoken about in all corners of Trinidad and Tobago. That made it easier to wake up every morning rearing to go to continue doing the job that God had put him here to do, with all the pride in the world.

Alas, Claude has also passed on to repair all those old Land Rover jeeps in heaven under the guidance of our Lord and Master. I know he is being sheltered under His wings of love for eternity. He is also sorely missed right here, but I am now placing him in this community's hall of pillars of my town. Thank you, Claude. By the way he was the younger brother of Mr. Victor "V. J." Joseph, another stalwart of our town. I am sorry to say here that his property happened to be one of the casualties involved in the takeover of lands by this administration with the purpose of the runway extension for the A. N. R. Robinson airport.

Mr. Ewitts Douglas was exceptional with Ford cars, and I cannot say where or who he learnt his skill from but as far as I know he was great with Fords. He was head mechanic at the McAnarney Ford Motor Company, which was located at the corner of Milford Main Road and Mt. Marie Road in Scarborough Tobago.

One of the first things I could remember about Ewitts and Arnold, was that they lived two blocks from me in Canaan, and during my Bishop's High school days when I needed a ride to school, because of the negligence of my father, (spoken about in my first book "The Shadow of Fear and Hunger",) if I got to their home before they left for work, I had a choice of two cars in which to travel.

Arnold, on the other hand, worked At Tobago Motors Northside Road, Calder Hall, he was the best in his field with Volkswagen and Nissan cars and elevated himself to head mechanic there.

Not much can be said about those two men except that both were very soft spoken and very reliable at their jobs. Arnold got married to one of uncle Cs daughters, I don't think they had any children, and Ewitts, as far as I know, has one child, a boy who is the owner of a guesthouse located at the corner of John Gorman Street, Bon Accord, Tobago.

Sadly, they have both passed on, and like I said with Claude, I'm sure they are in Ford and Volkswagen heaven doing their needful at repairs, while sheltered under the wings of our Lord and Master mechanic Jesus Christ. They too are sorely missed, but we know that their times were up and their jobs on earth were done, and it was time for their rest.

Chapter Eight

I love cars with a passion, I love to see a car look its best, well taken care of, shiny and lovely interior, and working at its best. So, I started out a small business buying used cars, one at a time, and repairing them for resale, my final tally of cars I bought and sold was fifty, including two five series BMWs and two Nissan Cefiros, I'm now driving number fifty-one, a brand-new Nissan X-Trail.

I recall an occasion when I bought this used car, a Nissan Datsun sixteen, PBO 4215, from Mr. Joseph Winchester, knowing it needed bodywork. So, after consulting this garage at Canaan, Mr. Omil John's, I decided to give him my car to do the job. No contract was signed, but a handshake was the way things were done in those days, hoping that each party kept his word.

There were rust spots on all four doors, fenders and the lower panels on both sides, those being the main areas for repair and painting. The estimated time for completion was two weeks. After two weeks I had money ready to pay for my repaired car and was eager to see the finished product.

I went to collect my car and was met with animosity, not even having the slightest idea where it came from. I told him I had the money agreed to and I had come to pay him and get my car, but he said the car was not ready to be delivered. I asked when it would be ready, and he said within two more days. In the meantime, *"a little bird"* whispered to me that the problem was all about money. He felt he had undercharged me. I had no way of knowing then the true nature of the job he had done.

After two more days I went to get my car to find out that it was ready but there was no battery in it. It cost me the price of a battery to remove my car from his garage.

At first glance it pleased me to see the job he did, until after a few days I began to see spots emerging all around where most of the repair work had been done. After two weeks of washing and preparing my car for sale I noticed bubbles began appearing all around the car, I had to call off potential buyers, that was when I started to become upset, I think any reasonable person would have been.

I made the decision to have another opinion as to the appearance of my car because from what I saw that was not what I had paid for. On closer inspection we came to realize that it was a not a well-done job and restoration had to be done all over again. To the tune of twice what I had paid the first straightener, Mr. John. I had to sacrifice and do it all over.

So, we started over to find something we never would have believed was done by the man who was supposed to have repaired my car. He had taken a hammer to my car's four doors and panels and bashed them in and placed wet cement bags all over the doors and panels and then covered the wet cement paper with filler. He did a wonderful job of getting everything smooth and presentable for painting, deceiving me in such a big way.

All of this came to light when the new guy, Mr. Lennox "Lil ting" Quamina, started to investigate the bubbles all around my car. Looking at my car I wanted to cry to see all my money go down the drain for wet cement paper.

One day while Lennox was at work on my car the first straightener, Omil John, came by to investigate why my car was at this other garage. After watching Lennox scrape off the cement paper and old filler from the doors and panels for a while, he asked him why he was doing such a good job on my car if he didn't see he had given me what I deserved. And this is a true experience, this really happened, borne out of spite, envy and jealousy.

I say it like that because I ask no one for anything, so nobody knows when I need something or when I don't have something. One of my dad's early lessons that I will never forget. And that's when I knew how some people saw me. I was always trying to improve myself, because I knew about growing up not having anything, so I was always going about my business, not bothering anyone with what I was doing.

I am positive that if the parents of this young man were aware at the time, they too would not believe that their son was capable of doing something as despicable as that, and for no specific reason. I never said or did anything to this young man to deserve treatment like that, otherwise I would not have taken my car to him in the first place. They might have even gone further by disowning him as their son, because they were God fearing people. I also know that God never sleeps, and He pays all debts, not with money, but in kind, according to how everyone works. To tell you the truth I really think Mr. John is still being paid for his actions, even today.

I was saved from a prison term that day, because the call to urinate came just before Mr. Omil John came to the new garage on a bicycle he borrowed, as he got news that my car was there. He had no knowledge that I was nearby, so God was there for me again. When I returned, I was told that he had been there and what he had said. I picked up a piece of iron and ran out to the road to see how far he had gone but I did not see him, he would have tasted it that day, that iron would have been his dose of multi-vitamin for that day. Just the thought running around in my head that he had done that before to other car owners, made me want to hurt him and change the course of his life with a hospital visit.

So, this story was just to show that not all the straighteners were the same. The thing is, justice was not served in that case, but I got my car about three weeks later and sold it for a small profit, even counting the time lost.

By the way, the despicable straightener is from right around Block 22 on the main road in Canaan, he turned out to be the worst straightener and painter in this entire village, and eventually everyone found out about him, and it put him completely out of business. it is said what goes around, comes back around, it's so true. I gave all the credit to Mr. Lennox Quamina for the wonderful job he did on my car's restoration.

When I first spoke to him, he was swamped with work, that was my reason for my approaching Mr. Omil "despicable" John. I gave Lennox all the recommendations when anyone asked about getting work done as beautiful as mine.

When you have some people doing their best to uplift a community, like Lennox did, you have some doing their best to pull it down. A "bent" pillar like that we could definitely do without.

But one bad apple would not spoil this bunch. Choose wisely. It also reminds me of my adopted motto: "Good Work or None."

Chapter Nine

There was this not so middle-aged lady who took her time to master her craft as a baker. Her temperament was that of a most tolerable person with a very sharp tongue. She would not think twice to let you know what she thought of you and the rest of your family, if it came to that.

She would usually wake very early to start her baking. In those days the bakers used a big dirt oven with two arches. The back arch for scraping out the ashes left from the fire set to heat the oven, and the front arch for taking out the baked product.

There were no temperature gauges to signify the heat in the oven, but with a sixth sense the baker could tell if the heat was too much or not enough. She would know the timing for her bread or coconut tart or bhajan as the case might be. My main interest in this case is coconut tart and bhajan, two of my favorites, both include coconut, (by the way, a bhajan is a delicacy made with flour, coconut and sugar, shaped like a small cucumber, but it's all about the taste).

I'm talking about Ms. Adina Roberts, for me the best coconut tart and bhajan maker in the world, she made a tasty mauby too and I would wait in line for both. The mauby was where my story is going full speed ahead.

In those days' mauby bark, from which the drink was derived, was sold at the market at Scarborough. Ms. Adina would have to either have someone buy it for her or get to town and buy it herself. It took time and money to produce her mauby for sale with the right taste.

It is every business person's aim it's to sell whatever the merchandise to make a profit, and Ms. Adina had the same idea. After boiling the mauby bark and doing her measurements, she would then know how much she would be able to sell to make profits on everything she sold at her parlor.

The mauby bark itself is a bitter blend so after boiling it she had to measure the bitterness so if she added water to a certain amount, it would not be bitter anymore. Then the sugar was added so when it was tasted all you taste is mauby sweet enough to have ice added to make the drink complete. In these modern times the mauby is sold in bottles already measured and sweetened, so you can just add water to your taste.

Ms. Adina had her parlor near to our old recreation ground where all the sports were being played so she would have visits from thirsty boys and girls all day every day, each with a different desire. Mine was the big glass; a twelve cents mauby and a twelve cents bhajan, maybe now and then I would buy a tart instead of the bhajan, but I cannot hide it I was a bhajan lover to my heart, and Ms. Adina knew that. So, it became a daily pattern or I should say as long as I had money.

Her measurement of bhajan with mauby became very evident and knowing how to not have one finish before the other was her masterpiece. But one day I started noticing that my mauby always finished before my bhajan, I would have a half of my bhajan in my hand and all the mauby would be gone.

In those days the ice truck would bring the ice to all the businesses early to start their day, it was sold by blocks. the seller would lift it out of the truck, held with a huge pliers type tool, and place it in the sink outside her window where it would melt without making any mess in her parlor, it weighed about fifty pounds. She would use an ice pick and chip the ice to fill the glasses.

Anyway, this day came, and I had enough of eating my bhajan without mauby because of too much ice filling up the glass so I ordered my bhajan and mauby and as Ms. Adina started chipping the ice I calmly said:

"Ms. Adina, can you please give me the ice in my hand, you fill up the glass with so much ice I do not have enough mauby to drink while eating my bhajan, I finish the mauby too fast no matter how I try to stretch it."

She was taken by surprise, so she said: "You can't tell me how to sell my mauby, you damn outta place."

I just said to her: "I know you saving the mauby to make more money but you spoiling my taste buds, and I can't eat my bhajan with the ice."

Then she said: "Is because you too damn rude to come here to tell me how to sell my mauby".

I left it at that, but I guess her conscience bothered her a bit because she knew my situation with my dad and me, and as I started to leave, she called out to me to come and get some more mauby, she gave me another half glass. The next time I went to her parlor she just watched me and smiled, we were best of friends from that day.

Later in life after she retired and closed her shop, I was one of the people who would go to her home and order bhajans and make gifts to my bhajan loving friends. She had no children or relatives that I knew of, and very little resources other than her famous bhajan skill, so I just wanted to help her in any way I could. The loving soul she was.

She encouraged a young lady to come and help her make my orders of bhajans so she wouldn't die without leaving her legacy with one of the youths of the village. Eventually I did help some more by donating to the home for the aged where she was a tenant, she passed away peacefully, well loved by all in this community. May her soul rest in peace! What a personality eh? Another pillar that should not be forgotten.

Chapter Ten

I must give a shout out to my dearly departed friend Esau George. He was a small man, about five feet six inches tall, brown skinned, some would say close to handsome, depending on how you look at him. He weighed about one hundred and fifty pounds, and as far as I know he never had any children. He was married to one of Mr. Calvin Chapman's daughters, she passed away before him, and he lived into his nineties. May he rest in eternal peace. He was no "big name" in the village, but because he was us footballers' best friend, I must pay my respects.

I got to know Esau since in the early fifties, when he worked at Crown Point Airport, because my dad worked there at the same time. He was always a quiet man going about his business at his own pace. When a passenger came to the airport to travel Esau was the man to take care of the bags after they came off the scale. He would put them on the cart, and when the cart was full it was then pushed out of the building to the waiting aircraft.

When the aircraft arrived his job was reversed, he helped to take them off the aircraft onto the same cart to be taken into the building for the owners to claim their bags with the corresponding tags, before leaving.

But there was another side to Esau, he loved shoemaking. I can truly tell anyone that the saying about a shoemaker never wears a good pair of shoes is a myth, as far as Esau was concerned. His shoes were always looking top of the line. Anyone watching him walk will undoubtedly know that walk came from the nice shoes he always wore.

Another aspect of Esau was his pleasant demeanor, he was just a special individual. Going into his shop after work to have anything done, he was comforting in conversation, young people today would say he was "cool". He made you feel real comfortable chatting with him, he made you feel like you had no problems at all.

He was the young footballers' best friend; I can remember clearly how he would take our busted shoes and make them so comfortable for playing again. The only way he would have any problem with a shoe is if he didn't have the right size of last to fit it. Apart from that he was in his comfort zone in his shop.

And he did not only repair shoes, when we took our busted football to him, he just smiled and told us what time to return to collect it. And his timing was impeccable, every time, knowing the urgency about the game. In those days of laced up balls with rubber tubes inside we had Esau as our factory maintenance for footballs, just as the gas station owner Recto, would see us often too. because after Esau finished with the ball, we would steal a bike most times to head for the gas station to patch the tube and pump it up. Because according to where it burst the tube might need to be patched, before we could get to play any ball again.

Esau will be sorely missed, especially when I pass by where his shop used to be, and the memories decide to hit me. He was also my rock when my dad did his disappearing acts. He was just four buildings east of my home, so Esau was my first stop when I was alone. He was someone I could depend on for kind words and understanding. Those were the best days, and men like Esau made them so, may his soul rest in eternal peace shaded under God's wonderful wings of love. One gracious pillar if I ever knew one.

Chapter Eleven

No input is too small to mention as they all contributed to the enhancement of our village. For instance, our first mail person was a lady named Ms. Dress. She controlled the Canaan Post Office which was situated on the Milford Road, three houses east of George Street just next to where Reeves Louis had his shop, right by where there was a Long Mango (Mango Vere as Trinidadians call it) tree. I used to pitch marbles there under that tree. That is a famous spot also because until recently it was the home of First Citizens Bank (FCB), Canaan branch, and now boasts one of the

This is the site of the first post office in the 1950s, then a tailor shop, then FCB, and now the newest Supermarket in Canaan.

largest supermarkets in Cannan.

Ms. Dress' successor was her own daughter, Ms. Gertrude Ranjitsingh. She became our post office attendant and served this community with the expertise of a true professional, well-educated and well respected within the whole village. She lived in the same building as the post office with her family of four boys and two girls, Elgin, one of her sons, was also a member of the Somerset football club. I think there was another son, I think his name was Hugo, but I was not familiar with him until much later, as he was the eldest.

If I remember correctly because of the post office being at that location the first telephone booth was put right there on that same compound. Later on, one of the best tailors had his shop there, he was known as Boss Solo. I honestly think that Boss Solo was the tailor that Lord Nelson sang about in his big hit "King Liar". This man was that good a tailor, *"just show him the corner where anyone pass"* and he could make that person a perfect fitting suit. Because of his prominence in his field at that time, young men flocked to his shop to be taught. He taught them so they would carry on his legacy after he passed on. I am sorry to say that only two names come to my mind as students of the Boss, they are Joel Daniel and "Saga" Williams. They followed in the Boss' footsteps very well and turned out to be great tailors, the Boss would have been very proud.

Just off the corner of George Street, in a structure that still stands today, we were fortunate to have Mr. Joshua Sandy's, shop on that spot. My information was that he sold flour, rice, sugar and other foodstuff and rum there, with emphasis on the rum. He would bring in the rum from Trinidad and with his own expertise concoct his own brand and with the customers' taste buds being satisfied he made it worth his time and business was great. Reeves Louis eventually occupied that same structure with his entire family after making some adjustments to the living facilities.

Mr. Joshua Sandy, was the father of Wolsey, Bevon, Shiela, and Ignacius, all pillars in themselves

Chapter Twelve

In my last chapter I mentioned Bevon Sandy, one of Joshua's four children, who by the way, is ninety-five years old as I write, thank God for his longevity.

He had a desire to be a fireman, he joined the service at an early age and made a vow to diligently serve his country, and be the best he could be, exemplifying the virtues of the saying, "it's not what your country can do for you, but what you can do for your country." He moved up through the ranks and was afforded a scholarship to study further, in the United Kingdom. On his return he was made a Commander and put in charge of a Fire Station in Trinidad. He worked there until his retirement then returned to Tobago to rest with peace and tranquility having served as a top man in the Trinidad and Tobago fire service to his pleasure.

Another example of excellence showing the tenacity of the man, and by extension, being a native of our village, I must give him the total admiration and respect he's due, setting the example for all the younger ones to follow, putting country before self is in my opinion the actions of a true patriot.

Bevon's sister, Shiela Sandy, became Shiela Crooks, the loving wife of Mr. Bertie Crooks and they had two children Pamela and Kenny Crooks, both deceased now. Ms. Shiela, as she was lovingly called, went into the retail business, following in her father's footsteps, and had an establishment on the corner of Milford Road and Robert Street.

The structure is still standing today, having gone through one of the disasters of our time hurricane Flora, during the storm a young lady who was sheltering at the front of her shop, became an unfortunate victim because the awning broke away and covered her and she got a very serious injury. Thank God for his mercies she is still alive today, but she walks with a limp in memory of that fateful day.

Ms. Sheila was another pioneer who served her country with pride and devotion. May she rest in peace.

Mrs. Sheila Sandy- Crooks' establishment, at Robert Street Canaan, opposite Stumpy's Emporium

There was also Mr. Wolsey Sandy, Bevon's Brother who was also a shopkeeper not too far away from his sister Ms. Shiela. it seemed to run in the family, but they all had the motivation to serve their community and they were all much appreciated assisting the village to an easier way of life, which is what happens when you have everything you need in proximity. I give him a thank you for his service.

In those days it was hard work selling foodstuff and other items; they were even given a half day to rest every Thursday, the Government made it mandatory. Every item like flour, sugar, rice, potatoes, saltfish, salt, butter and other stuff like those had to be put on a scale and weighed, even onions just came in bulk, so having to do all that extra work a half day was designated for every shopkeeper to rest. This half-day was known as *"Shop Sabbath"* among the locals.

From one family there were five pillars, whether you want to believe it or not, some people are born with a silver spoon, whereas some have spoons thrust at them and they spend almost a lifetime trying to find out what type of spoon they have. But this family took to business like ducks to water. Thank you to all the Sandys for their meaningful contribution.

There was also a shopkeeper at Gaskin Bay Road, Bon Accord, the late Massa Cooke, it's the only name I know him by. He was a shop owner and the father of one of the fastest sprinters of that time, Mr. Fritz Cooke.

Then there was the late Mr. Neville *"Chico"* George, one of the first truck owners of our village. He lived next to another pioneer, the late Mr. Sento Lindsay, another shop owner on the main road near Silk Cotton Street, Bon Accord. Then there was the late Mother Streakly, another shop owner near to the airport. Mother Streakly's husband was a guy called *"Wahbeen",* I've known him for donkey years and that was the only name I knew him by.

Chapter Thirteen

Mrs. Hilda Patrick, the owner of "First and Last" parlor was another businesswoman who baked all her delicacies for sale out of her own dirt oven. She specialized in Coconut tarts and bhajan and her own tasty mauby, by the name of her establishment you would understand that she was exclusive through her location. She was the first spot to get something to eat as you came from Storebay or the airport, and the last spot if you came from Canaan on your way to the beach. The advantage of this was people did a lot of walking in those days so coming or going to or from the beach you would get thirsty and/or hungry.

I remember her husband very well, he worked at the Crown Point airport along with Esau and my dad and because he made me receive one of the *"finest lickings"* from my dad. The licking came about because he loaned me some kerosene one night while I was out with some other boys, catching crabs without my father's permission, (story related in my first book, *"The Shadow of Fear and Hunger."*)

The late Ms. Enid Horsford was another baker from Bon Accord.

Another baker was a Mr. Charlie James who lived at St Cyr Street. He owned a bakery that supplied bread and cakes for our village. and one of his sons has continued that tradition today, *"like father, like son".*

Obliquely opposite to the site of the James' bakery there is now a business place called Western Plumbing and Electrical Supplies Limited, where we have a most friendly staff of efficiently qualified attendants for all our plumbing and electrical needs.

Ms. Audrey George from Bon Accord was another small enterprise entrepreneur who catered mostly to the children that attended Bon Accord Primary School. She was armed with the knowledge that many of their parents would be away at work and might not be able to attend to them, according to the times their jobs afforded them when it was lunch time. Many of these parents would give their children money for lunch, that's where Ms. Audrey came in. She knew all the treats the kids loved, and being knowledgeable about baking her specialties, she went into business. She had a small booth erected right on the corner in front of the school and was always ready for lunchtime.

Now everybody has their special delicacy that they excel in, and Ms. Audrey was no different. She was skilled in making Roly Poly, Rock Cakes, Sponge Cakes and the cream of the crop was her bread and Acra (made from saltfish fried in soft dough) it was to die for. Then to add to the full lunch there was her mauby. Or maybe a red Solo and a Roly Poly.

Anyhow you put it together she was at a convenient spot and the kids never stopped coming. If I'm not mistaken, Ms. Audrey, as a single mother with five kids was able to send all of them through high school from right there, if that was not good enough, then I do not know what is. It just goes to show the genius of used talent, and it says also, "it's not what you do, it's how you do it".

And her kids weren't any disappointment, they all made something of themselves. They all qualified themselves academically to have good sustainable jobs, which is a credit to each one of them. Kudos go to Ms. Audrey George, and to those kids who didn't let all her hard work and dedication go to waste, I do applaud that family.

Another family I want to recognize here is none other than my good neighbors the Huntes, who became the Pollards and had a thriving business which reigned throughout the decades even up until today. I'm talking about Ms. Martha Hunte who married Mr. Norris Pollard and as Mrs. Martha Pollard weaved a solid business in trafficking fresh produce

This structure which still stands today with a few modern renovations, was the site of the Pollards shop, Wolsey Sandy's Shop and Esau's Shoemaker Shop at different times during my town's history. It's a store for school supplies and uniforms now.

and livestock and along with the sale of shop goods made it a complete success.

I would refer to them as *"a power couple"*. When I first knew that couple Mrs. Martha Pollard would buy stuff from the villagers here, things like dried coconuts, a goat, sheep, chickens, crabs, peas and corn, vegetables or anything she thought could sell for a profit at the market in Trinidad. Norris would stay in their shop at Canaan while Ms. Martha would make her trips to Trinidad to do her trafficking.

Even in this modern day one might notice from time to time a pick-up truck would pass on the main road blowing its horn to attract attention. They do that so anyone who has animals like cows, goats and sheep can do some business with them. They buy here and take them to Trinidad to sell for a profit.

Well, Mrs. Pollard was one of the pioneers who started that trend along with Mr. and Mrs. Deacon and Marjorie Roberts of Robert Street, the other power couple. I've heard stories from traders with both traffickers who complained that they lost money to them because they would weigh their chickens, get the cost for the chickens, and was promised the money on consignment when they returned, but never got paid when they returned to Tobago. The reason being the chickens was sick or old and died on the journey, said the traffickers, so they never got the chance to sell to make any money. There were some disgruntled patrons, but it all boils down to the profit and loss margin, in business it goes with the territory.

Earlier I recognized Ms. Juanita Hunte who I rode to school with along with Mr. Russel Martineau, she is Mrs. Martha Pollard's niece, of Antiguan Heritage. They were great businesspeople coming from humble beginnings. The Hunte family are still in business today with two huge groceries on this Island. The groceries are run by the indefatigable Mr. Kenworth Hunte, Juanita's younger brother, and his lovely wife Melanie, still going strong decades later.

I admire their tenacity, dedication and business acumen. Kudos go out to that family, and I wish them many more fruitful years developing our community to its fullest potential.

Chapter Fourteen

There is a significant gentleman I must mention in this stroll down memory lane because he had prominence in this town and was well respected; Mr. Duport George.

I was told he was a councilman in an earlier time, but I knew him as a businessman with control over that corner at the four roads junction at Bon Accord. The man had a rum shop, foodstuff shop and a parlor. He meant that if you were at that corner, he must be able to sell you something.

That corner was always busy, because the bus stop was, and is still there along with the remains of Duports' parlor.

Above left; the remains of Duport's Parlor, and above right; the still functioning refurbished bus stop.

And when you needed a taxi and/or whether you were sheltering from the sun or rain you did it at Duports' business place.

I was told he started with a little covered over shed, selling some biscuits he baked himself. He later introduced Cowie's bakery products along with his own homemade mauby, and carbonated drinks supplied by the Bottlers Limited. Yeah, we had our own Juicy factory at Shaw Park, the building is still there, run down, but still standing.

I was told that the youths of the area played football in the Bon Accord estate area, that was before they made the recreation ground, so they had to come to Duport's for refreshments. He was the only establishment around there at the time. Eventually he expanded and the Four Roads corner became his.

Like I said, I must mention this man because of the influence he had on the community. Unfortunately, he passed away not long after he got my attention. I was more familiar with his soft-spoken wife, whom I knew as Mrs. Mattie George. She was a friendly soul and as far as I knew was nice to everybody. Her daughter, who I knew as Ms. Baby had the same temperament, her husband, however, was another matter. Mrs. Baby James eventually inherited the businesses at that corner and continued to flourish until her retirement, her kids did not have the future of that business as an option, so none of them followed in her footsteps.

The thing was, Ms. Baby's husband Police Constable Charlie James' path crossed with mine at one time and I got the better of him, just by sheer luck. I had a job driving a fish van owned by Mr. Charlie Jones, a Barbadian jockey who had a fish trade going on here from Milford Bay. Jones owned three trawler vessels and a jeep, which I drove, without a permit, I was 16 years old. As my dad owned a car, I was taught how to drive it really early, before I was sixteen years old. And because of the man my dad was I had to learn how to drive well, otherwise it was blows. My level of ability helped me to get the job.

A *"little bird"* told Jones that Constable James would be setting up a roadblock the following morning to catch me driving the jeep. So, the next morning Jones took the wheel and put me in the tray to sit with the fishermen. I had no idea why, and didn't ask him anything, he was my boss.

We came to the roadblock and up walked the constable and said: "Where is the regular driver of this vehicle?"

Jones said: "You are looking at him."

James said: "Not you, I know it's your vehicle, I'm talking about the boy who drove it yesterday."

Jones replied: "I drove my vehicle yesterday, is there anything else officer I have fish to sell."

Charlie James was embarrassed facing five other officers who just looked at him with total disdain.

Charlie James said: "No nothing else, you can go".

We left them standing around looking stupid. After we had driven about five miles Jones stopped and called me to do my job.

"Joe Joe", considered one of the *"baddest"* policemen to pass through this village, heard the story about my driving and how I got away with it so he took it upon himself to get revenge anyway he could. I only knew this police officer as *"Joe Joe",* I think his surname was Providence. He rode a motorbike and wanted to lock up everybody who he didn't like, just another "bad egg" with a showing off attitude.

He had me running away every time he came around, because he said he just didn't like me. He told everyone once he caught me, he would lock me up and he would find something to charge me with. So, whether I was playing football or just liming, once he came around, I had to disappear from the area. But he never caught me, I saw to that.

Regardless of these instances my teenage years into my twenties and most of the young men like me, were not interested in any lawlessness and crime. We were focused on learning something worthwhile to better ourselves for the life we would have in the future.

There were those of us who learned a trade, thinking about being self-sufficient and independent. That was how we had new carpenters, masons, electricians and plumbers, in our village. Then the same young men who played football with me during the afternoons, after they were finished with their trade for the day, were the same young men who played steelpan with me at night.

At one time the complete tenor-pan line up of *Old Oak Starlift Steel Orchestra* were footballers, there was Boysie *"Gango"* Waldron, Ephraim *"Tokes"* Dearie, the best goalkeeper in Tobago in Prescot *"Preco"* Sandy, two defenders in Gango and Tokes and I, Ken G. Gordon a forward. There were others in the band, like Pernell Thomas, another defender, on cello, and our midfielder Rupert *"Rupee"* Franklin on bass, all Somerset players. This is how we were thinking around that time, we were always too busy to get into trouble. It reminds one of the old saying, *"the devil finds work for idle hands to do".*

With most of our thought processes like that there was a minimum of even petty crime in our village. We had some differences of opinion, little scuffles now and then, cursed a few obscene (bad) words, rode our bicycles without lights, yes, that was breaking the law at one time, but crime was not prevalent here in our village.

There were no knife fights and cutlass choppings, with the exception of that one occasion with Mr. Joseph James when he lost his right hand at the wrist, and most definitely no guns, and no gangs. And most of the time, if and when, any of those fights did occur, the next day those involved would meet, with a third party, and discuss, and everyone would get back to normal. That was how we lived in our village, that way everyone made themselves useful in one way or another to the benefit of all in the community.

Chapter Fifteen

Staying with Canaan I recall that chubby contractor and revolutionary character none other than the big man himself, the illustrious Mr. Harris Desvignes, of Guy Street. I have always admired this man for his authority in the way he conducted his business. He singlehandedly crafted out a concrete business where he manufactured concrete blocks, inverts and cylinders, and was instrumental in procuring contracts with the government in charge of Tobago at the time, I think it would have been either The County Council or the Ministry for Tobago affairs. I'm not quite sure if he supplied Trinidad too, he might have, knowing the stature of the man.

As far as I could see he was all about community spirit. Most of the houses being built around that time would have been with either Tapia, a mixture of mud and straw, the bark of the cabbage tree or noggin, (explained in my first book *"The Shadow of Fear and Hunger"*). So, in order to alleviate the citizenry of going that route he would sell them concrete blocks for their homes and inverts for their drains.

The cylinders were also used locally for roads to properties in the village as well as exported to other villages. This man was a genius. I can see him now, always well dressed with his shirt in his pants, unless he wore a shirt jack, wearing work boots and shirt pocket bulging with his pack of cigarettes. What vision he must have had to sit and put something like that together, he must have been putting himself in other's shoes to come up with that idea.

He also had trucks and a backhoe for loading the products and transporting them to wherever they were needed.

I saw it with my own two eyes, wherever there was a road being cut or a bridge being constructed Mr. Desvignes' products were there. I put him in the same category as John Grant for taking the initiative; coming up with the idea and making it happen. I could just see him relishing the final product that came from what he put together in his head.

I can remember his driver's name too; we called him John *"La Croix"* Quamina. He worked a steady job bringing the gravel and cement and taking the finished product to customers wherever they were. Desvignes also hired other workers from the village to manufacture the products he became famous for. So, he was also instrumental in creating jobs for the villagers.

He also dabbled in horse racing, he had a couple of horses; *Play the Game* and *Whistling Rufus*. For him the interest was not so much in him being a winner, but being in the game of racing for the fun of it, like exhaling from the pressures of his responsibilities, a day for himself. Mr. Harris Desvignes was an essential pillar in our community.

Nothing is written in stone, and anyone can be what they want to be, all that is needed is ambition, determination and aspiration. Always look within yourself and find out what makes you feel comfortable and do the research into whatever makes you feel comfortable and employ yourself in that field. This way it's not work because you would be in your comfort zone and very willing to tackle whatever comes with the territory of your choice. Anything other than that makes you look like *"a square peg in a round hole"*, and would be no joy at all, just frustration and stress, and nobody needs that.

Chapter Sixteen

What I know of Mr. Siebert Chapman, better known as Uncle C's, personal life might be very little, but I am fully aware of the significant impact he had on our community. My knowledge started late one night while looking for something different to eat. I was driving at the time and the company I was with insisted we go to Crown Point to Uncle C's establishment and we would find what we were looking for, so we went. The boss was right we did find what we were looking for that night and every other night after that when we needed to eat something different.

He established himself as the place to go when you needed something nice to eat. I remember him for a really tasty fried chicken and fried fish anytime I went to his place I got the same great taste in his fish and chicken. I blame him for instigating the romance between my second daughters' mother and me. It's a short story of parental abuse causing a daughter to take matters into her own hands.

I was at the time living In Trinidad and met this young lady and fell hard for her. It was 1974 and I was working at American Stores driving a truck delivering furniture to all the outlets throughout Trinidad. I loved my job, anyway, after meeting this young lady I went to her home to meet her family after a while. Her mother was very kind to me but her father was simply a jackass. He told me he didn't like any Tobagonian for his daughter, I understood his attitude about me, nothing new to hear from a Trinidadian. I heard it quite a few times while living in Trinidad, but the worst part was how he treated the rest of the family when I visited my girlfriend. He went on the warpath just cursing and abusing everyone within the home, so I decided to come back to Tobago and forget all about her, and I did just that.

While I was in Tobago, I was getting phone calls from her about coming to Tobago to see me which I did not encourage because of the behavior of her father. I thought *"out of sight out of mind"*, but this was more like *"absence makes the heart grow fonder"*. It so happened that the day came when she really did come to Tobago, and this is where Uncle C took over. I was at work that day, I got a phone call from someone at the Crown Point airport that a young lady asked him to call me at work.

From the time I heard him say at the airport I just knew right away who it was, so I asked my foreman for some time off and I went to the airport to meet this young lady. It was around 11.00 am when I got to the airport, and there she was, in the flesh.

I took her across the street to Uncle C's, a stone's throw from the airport, to try and talk her out of what she had in mind to do, but she left Trinidad with her mind made up and Uncle C being right there just made it so much easier. He had everything just waiting to be ordered so we ordered eats and drinks and spent the rest of the day at the beach, that one day my second daughter was created as nine months later I had my second lovely daughter, compliments of Uncle C's establishment. She's now the grandmother of my first great grandson. If I was around, to have the privilege to name her, because I was living in Tobago, I would have tried to name her after Uncle C in some way, just a name beginning with a "C." One more pillar who left his mark for all to see.

Chapter Seventeen

Another one of the establishments that sprang up in Canaan around the last 25 or 30 years and keeps getting stronger all the time was the brainchild of a man who we just know as *"South"*. I know him as a carpenter by trade, with the tenacity and the ambition to make a better life for himself. What started off as the recreation club at Canaan eventually turned out to be a name well known throughout Trinidad and Tobago. Anywhere you go now, and you mention Block 22, the smallest child can explain where to find it.

"South" owned the recreation club and being involved with card games, anyone familiar with that type of night life will tell you that those games can go on for days for any one session, depending on the funds that are circulated on any given night. It is more of a nighttime activity because workdays get in the way of those who are really in love with those card games, and the funds needed to get involved in any one of the games must be had from a job of some kind. There is Gin Rummy, Patience, Go to Pack, Whappie and Poker, just to name a few.

There are still times when one session of games would last all weekend and during that time the only recess that players get is in relieving themselves in the washroom. Think about it, a player comes into the club on a Friday after he's been paid with his fat paycheck burning a big hole in his pocket, and he is eager to have some fun playing any game of his choice, that game could be one on one or within a group, as long as you abide by the club rules of any game you are free to play. By the way, the man in charge of the club, known as the *"Cassa"*, is always there to oversee fair play and to control all the games legitimately. In other words, he is like the referee, like in a boxing ring. He controls all the games happening because the games are taxed for upkeep and maintenance of the club.

Having explained what takes place at the club I can now continue to show you how all that coincides with the end product that connects to Block 22, and how it became as popular as it is today. Laying it all out; there are two types of guys who frequent recreation clubs, those with jobs and families and those without families and no jobs. The latter we call hustlers, and the hustlers equip themselves with all the cunning tools to relieve the workers of their hard-earned money. Most times making them work twice for their hard-earned money. I have known many families crumble and disintegrate because of those recreation clubs.

Having said all that, when the working-class men get trapped into losing their pay to the hustlers, they cannot go home empty handed to their families because they have mouths to feed. Hence, they eat and drink at the club until they can come up with some way to get back some money in their pockets to face the rest of the family. Some would borrow to try and win back, and some would borrow to go and face their family, facing up to their losses until next time. You had better believe that they sometimes spent the weekend at the club trying to recoup their losses, and you know how that would go over with the rest of the family.

While being in the club for all those hours they all had to eat and drink so *"South"* came up with the genius of an idea to start an addition to the club where he could sell fried fish and fried chicken with roast bake or bread as sandwiches, fries can be had also, with all the popular drinks available today. Because of his location a Lotto and Play Whe booth was also added to the establishment.

Then he added a bar license to his repertoire of accomplishments so he could offer alcoholic drinks to his customers and just like that Block 22, a semi all night eatery was established at the corner of Douglas Street and the Milford Road, Canaan. If it's a party weekend at Pigeon Point or Milford it becomes an all-night eatery, catering to the party goers too. Creating employment for almost ten families just like that.

And I can vouch for the taste of both the chicken and the fish, they are both delectable. Because of home grown garden seasoning, you get that same delicious taste every time you bite into a piece of chicken or fish. The taste of The Colonel's chicken cannot touch the taste of Block 22's chicken, I guarantee it. It tastes great! I always believe that common sense was made before books, and you do not

The recreation club Block 22 (2024) the home away from home for many whom are seeking the all night "lime".

have to be a university graduate with all kinds of initials behind your name to be a successful entrepreneur.

Mr. South can take a congratulatory bow in appreciation for his wonderful contribution to the enhancement of that famous corner. He is situated directly opposite to where the first Drug Store in the entire western half of Tobago was started. I take my hat off to the genius of the man. Thank you, sir!

Chapter Eighteen

It would be very remiss of me if I fail to mention the Jattans, who migrated to Tobago from Trinidad, somewhere around the mid-1960's, I do know that it was after hurricane Flora. My dad was fated to be their first landlord right here in Canaan. My dad had an unused parlor on our property and the Jattans were happy to live in it as a start to their new life in Tobago.

They were a family of six, father, mother and three sons, later a daughter came along, if my memory serves me right. Today, if anyone starts to talk about the wealthiest people in Tobago, they cannot leave out the Jattans, the names I can remember now are Pepe and Jesse, those two men own so much property on this island they cannot be left out of the conversation.

Coming from humble beginnings they worked hard to be who they are today, and I can vouch for their integrity with all my being. They came back to Canaan as proprietors as my wealthy neighbors, in the most influential way ever. I am not at liberty to divulge their ownership status on the island, but I can tell you it's extensive, take this author's word for it.

Pepe even owns a church and that just happened to come up in a conversation one day after he made the decision to stop the restaurant business he had at lower Scarborough. To give Jack his jacket, Jesse and Pepe own quite a few buildings in Scarborough and a few in Canaan and Lowlands too. I know I'm just scraping the surface here, but I had to mention them because they originated from Canaan.

One of the first prominent women to do business in Canaan was a lady I knew as Ms. Mabel; her building still stands on the original spot facing the entrance to Cove. She had a store selling what is considered as haberdashery; men's and women's clothing and cloth for sewing dresses, shirts and curtains. She was also into household items like spoons, cups, and plates.

Hardly anything was known about this lady, I never saw her outside of that store so my knowledge of her is very limited. She had a beautiful daughter named Dawn. And all I can remember about Dawn is her selling with her mother at their store, and at one time she drove a small car.

Chapter Nineteen

One of the stalwarts of this village was a guy who never asked for anything but to lend a hand ("len han") when he threw out his seine at Store Bay. Mr. Wilson Woods was that man, he was also the father of the owners of the guesthouse called Woodscastle, and a strong black man from whom I never heard an angry word unless his seine wasn't being pulled right.

The process of fishing with a seine is a lengthy one, it takes a lot of patience and about four or five men to start it off, I will endeavor to try and educate you on what I witnessed as a boy. First the seine is made with special twine, rope, cork and lead. The twine is for the net to trap the fish, there are different sizes of holes in the net, at the center of the net where the fish gets trapped the holes are small, so they can't escape once they get trapped.

At the side of the net are the bigger holes where the net which is attached to the rope for pulling into shore. The rope is attached to both sides of the net, the side with the cork and the side with the lead, so in pulling in the net there must be four sets of rope pullers. The cork side stays on top of the water and the side with the lead scrapes the sea floor, that leaded rope side is what cleaned the floor of the beach at Store Bay. I hope you have a better idea now about how the net was made and how it was used when fishing.

The other part is where the men are needed; first to lift the huge bundle of the net on to the small boat and then to let out the net within an arc, as the boat is rowed out to sea. While the men are taking out the net on the boat one of the men would throw out the net in the water surrounding any fish they can see beating. When the tide is a certain way the men can see the fish beating by the ripples on the surface, that's how they know there are fish to catch.

So, one end of the double rope is left on the shore to be held by men who are there to assist in the catch and the other end comes in when all the net is let out at sea to be received by another set of net pullers. There will now be four sets of pullers on shore, two sets on the cork and two sets on the lead, the cork pullers will be up high and lead pullers will be down low. At the end of the casting of the net it looks like the arc of a rainbow. The average length of the rope attached to the net is about one hundred and fifty feet. This is where the master steps in to orchestrate the pulling in of the seine.

At the top of the arc in the seine you could see there were fish by how the water rippled, so you know you caught fish. That's where the small holes are in the seine, to stop the fish from escape, unless the seine is not pulled in right. Now you must keep what got caught. Mr. Woods stepped in like the conductor of an orchestra telling everyone how he wanted the seine to be pulled, and who should hold and who should pull, it was a beautiful sight. All everyone was interested in was how hard the seine was to pull, because the harder it was to pull the more fish was in the catch, so it was more for everyone.

In the meantime, the fish were coming slowly but surely, and the pulling crowd got bigger all the time. And it was all because of the *"len han"system*; if you helped pull in the seine Mr. Woods rewarded every puller with fish, big or small, villager or visitor. When it was almost time for the seine to reach the shore and everyone anticipated what kind of catch was coming in, eagerly awaiting to see why they were helping. A bumper catch would have quite a few four and five pounders, mostly Cavally and Snappers (Red fish), but the main catch would be some big Jacks weighing about a pound each, and of course some herrings that could be used by other fishermen as bait.

Mr. Woods had done it again, this was the time everyone was waiting for, when he gave everyone their *"len han",* which came from the Jacks. The man had to make a living for his family; so, he shared the Jacks to all the pullers and kept the bigger fish for sale to some vendors who were right there waiting. Everybody was happy, especially Mr. Woods, and he was pleased that he was able to assist so many people's families in having a good nutritious meal from his contribution to the community. That was the type of man he was.

At one time he used a bicycle with carrier at the front where he would put his container with his Jacks and ride through the village blowing his conch shell to alert villagers, he had fish for sale. With his addition to the community with his essential contribution; aiding families feed their loved ones, what more can anyone ask of this pillar.

Mr. Wilson Woods also has something to be very proud of when he looks at what he started with only good intention in mind, trying to feed his family the only way he knew. He has made the way clear for tourists visiting from all over the world to have a relaxing swim at his old Store Bay with a clean sea bed. He made this possible by pulling his seine and having that lead on the bottom rope take all the stuff that was on the floor, and making Store Bay known worldwide as one of the most beautiful beaches in Tobago, along with Pigeon Point.

His character and love for his family has done wonders for this Island I draw others attention to his contribution to the well-being of this island. To me, it was the selfless action on his part that we of Tobago can now bow to his participation and can now say a hearty thank you for all he did, it truly inspires and shows the heroic quality of the man.

May the good Lord shelter him under His wings of love forever, he is sorely missed, gone but not forgotten. With pillars like those anyone would be able to conceive the possibility of the future we are in today.

Chapter Twenty

I want to talk about tradesmen, of which we had some really excellent carpenters. That was most evident after hurricane Flora. The recovery rate was so high that most villages were in awe when most of our homes were repaired in such a short time, and life had gone back to normal here in Canaan. Passersby would notice that the emergency tents that were erected at the recreation ground were disappearing one by one as homeowners went back to their original homes. I may not know much about personal lives of the carpenters of my village, but I have testimony to their competence and not only from the residents of the village but from other places they have worked.

After Flora, having all that extra work on their hands, they made sure that they took care of their home village first, before venturing beyond our borders to assist our neighbors. A few names come to my mind to mention; starting with Mr. Mack Bynoe, who lived on Guy Street, Canaan, who I felt, from seeing his work, was the best of them all. I heard it said that when someone had anything to construct, it was if he was busy with work at the time of the request and the time when he felt he would be available for that persons' job was too far away, that's when another carpenter would be approached.

The man was that great, and he wasn't a big talker, he let his handiwork speak for him. *"Some men were born to be great, and some would have greatness thrust upon them"*, Mr. Mack was born great. This pillar was a champion of his community, believe this writer when he says he can vouch for what he writes here. I stake my young writing career on everything that is said here, my word is me. Mr. Mack Bynoe has passed on and is with His Maker, and the genius of the man will be forever missed. *"He also came, saw, and conquered",* may he rest in eternal peace.

My second in line would be Mr. Leonard Chapman, of Bon Accord. He was one with a difference, to me, a carpenter with a *"chip on his shoulder"*, having personally dealt with him. I can only say from hearsay that he had some class in the way he worked but I cannot verify because of practical experience. He was my best friend's uncle, and they were very close, so I'll have to depend on his word and create a space for another pillar of our society.

Then there was Mr. David Roberts, of Robert Street Canaan, brother of Mr. Deacon Roberts, the trafficker, and son of Mr. Boatman Roberts who organized the early goat and donkey races at Robert Street. David was a good carpenter, and he was well sought out too, but he took the easy way out, and went into the service of the government for that easier and steady salary. That's how men measure themselves by different yardsticks and make decisions. One would say if he was that good why would he leave working for himself to go into the service of the government, and that was the criteria I used to put him third on my list.

I happened to have the need for a carpenter a couple of times, and I employed him. He worked to my satisfaction so I can vouch for his work, he lived near my home, and he has been an asset to our community. He was instrumental in rebuilding our community center after it was damaged by hurricane Flora. He was the man in charge of making sure everything was put back in its right place. And community work is volunteer work. What I am doing here is not for any specific award, it's just for my readers to ascertain the viable prospects who were contributors to the building of our town as it is today. So, I think Mr. David Roberts has been inducted as one of the pillars of our community. He too has passed on and is sheltering under the wings of love of the good Lord awaiting that great day.

Chapter Twenty-One

It would be remiss of me to neglect mentioning Mr. Frankie Latour who owned the largest estate in Canaan, the Golden Grove estate, with lands stretching from Buccoo Road on the north down to the Buccoo beach on the northwest to old Shirvan Racetrack on the east and bounded on the south by the Milford Road.

Almost every young man who lived at Canaan worked at Latour's estate at one time or the other. Even this writer did a one-week spell there for $2.65 a day picking up the fallen coconuts and filling up the tractor's tray to take into the compound to be cut up to make copra, (the kernels were dug out of the shell and put in the sun to dry) which was shipped to Trinidad to make coconut oil and soap at a factory in Laventille.

The money was small, and the hours were long, they were from 7.00am to 4.00pm, with a half hour for lunch. I had just left school without anything to show that I had even attended school. I was not fortunate enough to get a shot at the G.C.E. examinations, and after attending six different schools, (my story told in my first book, *"The Shadow of Fear and Hunger"*) I had no way of convincing any employer of my ability to compete with anyone for any type of job. So, I went to Mr. Frankie Latour.

I looked strong and that was all the criteria needed for this job. But after that week when I got paid, I looked at the money in my hand and something told me I could do much better at anything else, even if it meant staying at home.

When I'm in Trinidad, I would make it my duty to pass on the Eastern Main Road when passing through Laventille going to Port of Spain to get one of the sweetest smells I could get emanating from Tobago coconuts being processed for their special place in the world. Also, because Mr. Latour had so many cows and horses, on Fridays he would have the vet come to his plantation and check out a special animal before killing it for beef. He would help the village by giving them the opportunity to get his beef at a reduced price.

Whether you worked for him or not he and his sisters would cater for the villagers in this way, and it was greatly appreciated by all. Even after he died the sisters carried on the tradition. In conclusion I think it is safe to say that the criteria are met by Mr. Frankie Latour to add him to the collective pillars we have already acquired, for going above and beyond the barriers and boundaries to place his name among the elite. He also was called home a while back to be with his Maker and Lord of hosts to rest in His loving arms until that trumpet sounds.

Chapter Twenty-Two

We had a butcher in Robert Street, Canaan by the name of Mr. Albert *"Wapp"* Thomas, who had one child that I knew about, we went to school together for a time, his name was Melville *"Mello"* Thomas, we played football together for none other than the best team in Tobago at the time, I'm talking about Somerset Football Club. Back to the father; I cannot say how he got that nickname, but everybody called him Albert *"Wapp".* He was a racehorse enthusiast, but his main thing was that every Friday he had his butchering to do, to make a living to feed his family.

Apart from Mr. Latour's contribution with supplying meat for the village it was "Albert *Wapp's"* responsibility to serve his community with beef. It was customary for him because in those days nobody raised chickens as they do now, and beef was the staple meat for everybody's Sunday meal. Chickens were raised mostly for their eggs for breakfast and at for baking cakes for the seasons of Christmas and Easter. The thing I always tried to understand was why were they only killing off cocks for eating in those days and without cocks the hens could not have chickens.

Anyway, the times have changed and without chickens now there would no KFC or Church's Chicken, and a whole other industry would be in shambles. And now red meat is associated with raising the risk of diabetes, heart disease and stroke. I cannot doubt all that research, and I cannot say if it's because of less meat eaters that people are living longer these days, I'm just saying.

Anyway, kudos go out to Mr. Albert *Wapp* Thomas for his contribution to this community in supplying the entire village with meat and doing it without any complaint, and he would always throw in that piece of meat left in his hand after he weighed your order, count on it. The last thing I heard about his son Melo, is that he was in the USA living somewhere in Seattle, Washington, I wish him God's speed as I name his father one of the pillars of our village for his contribution to our society. Mr. Albert Wapp Thomas has passed on, but he is still sorely missed by everyone who had the distinct pleasure of dealing with the man. Sometimes I can still see him in my mind's eye riding that bicycle going home. I ask God to put his soul to rest and shelter him for eternity and beyond. May he rest in peace.

Chapter Twenty-Three

I have said nothing about our barbers, of which at the time I only knew one by the name of McAllister. I never knew his first name, but to just say that name everyone would know who it was you were talking about. I went to him every time I needed a haircut, just like everyone else, and it cost me nothing. Today it's a way of life for many young men in our village to open and run barbershops. In America they even made a movie about a barbershop. But I know I must mention him, apart from being a part-time barber, he was a steel-bender, and he was gainfully employed in the construction section at our Works Department in Scarborough.

He was a quiet sort of guy, and he was mentioned in my first book, *"The Shadow of Fear and Hunger",* he was the guy who shaved the area around the cut on my head to put the plaster on, after my father had blessed me with his shoe heel. He would also volunteer his services as a steel bender around the village. If in passing he noticed that you had a building under construction and you needed his services, if he had the time, he would help free of charge. He too has passed on and is sorely missed, but I know he's covered under the wings of love by our Savior until the trumpet sounds. Another pillar not to be forgotten for the quiet way he served.

Mr. Godfrey *"Flaps"* Trim was another one of our distinguished villagers who from my recollections worked at the Crown Point airport at around the same time as Mr. Esau George and was also a shoemaker by trade. I also remember the times he spent at our house playing cards with my father and others. Before there was a club, our house substituted as one. Flaps was a boisterous man; he was loud and always boastful. I think it was all because of his size he would put up that façade of strength to ward off attacks of any kind because he knew he was a softie. I would be in the bedroom trying to do my homework and his mouth would be the one I would hear the most. He was a small man about five feet five inches, weighing around one hundred and twenty pounds, that small, but you could not tell by his mouth, the way it flapped, I believe that was how he got his nickname. His job at the airport was the same as Mr. Esau's, both were responsible for taking care of the travelers' bags, going and coming, and after work he too would be repairing shoes for his customers.

"Flaps" had a history of eye problems and before you knew it, he was blind, but did you know his mouth never stopped flapping? We would go to check up on him and he would ask for a fight, even though he was blind. He was very jovial even in blindness and he was a joy to listen to after you got used to his way.

I do miss him very much since he passed on. He was someone I held on to as he was so closely associated with my father, having also worked with him at the airport. I never told anyone that was the reason I checked on him, but he was younger than my father and Esau, hence I expected him to be around longer, but he passed on before Esau. Life is funny sometimes. It is said that the best way to live one's life is to live each day to its fullest, that way you avoid having any regrets because tomorrow is promised to no one. So, instead of procrastinating by always leaving things for the next day over which you have no control, do it today and if and when tomorrow comes you have another opportunity to do some more. As my father used to say, *"the ripe limes are expected to fall from the tree",* but today the *"green limes"* fall before the *"ripe ones".* Nonetheless, I still enroll him in my tally of pillars of Canaan, and as always, I ask God to shade him under His wings of love, keeping him warm, and may his soul rest in eternal peace.

Chapter Twenty-Four

Earlier in my story I mentioned that pillars like Mr. John Grant and others left their legacy for us to build on. And others noticed the potential of doing businesses in this new town, starting with First Citizens Bank, who were here for a few years first and noticed how rewarding it was for their business, so they made it permanent by building their own structure. There were many others with the same opinion, we have Standard Furniture as well as Unique Furniture stores completely leaving out the town of Scarborough to partake of the pickings that can be had in my new town.

We are also blessed with a family of young men called the Warners, who have come into the business world in such a prominent way that my new town is showing the benefits significantly. They built some of the largest Supermarkets on our island, of course the largest one is in Canaan. They are called Penny Savers, and there are three to shop at.

West City (Penny Savers Mall) located at Canaan one of the most diverse shopping centres on the island of Tobago.

The one in Canaan is only a small part of the building complex they constructed called West City. There are several shops, including Western Union, Berry link for all your phone needs and an optician for all your eye care, naming just a few, housed in a modern two storied structure. There's even an escalator to the second floor to several shops. And they introduced the first self-opening doors in Tobago in their supermarkets.

In a truly comfortable setting right on the main road in Canaan, you can have access to two ATM machines right on the compound. The latest pharmacy to be opened is also situated on the ground floor of that same building. They have created a most enjoyable shopping atmosphere here in Canaan.

Along with Penny Savers we have two other supermarkets all three are within 150 meters of each other on Milford Road, Canaan.

And opposite to all of this there is Ansa Motors, for Honda, Mitsubishi and other popular brands of cars and trucks. If you feel like buying or trying out a new truck or car. Anyone can just cross the street and have all the convenience to shopping at Standards Furniture store if they feel like buying a living room set.

Talking about furniture reminds me that to have furniture there must be a home to put it in. We are blessed with four Hardware Stores for all our building needs, the oldest being Kissoon's Hardware at Bon Accord. I knew the owner from inception coming from Trinidad with his family just in time to acquire a piece of our paradise, a part of Killgwyn's estate. He had the idea that he could help transform this area with lumber and house building material, and he did.

he was a gentleman in the truest sense of the word. and I can back up that with the memory of the man, because he helped me when I came back from the USA and started to build my apartments, I went to him with a proposition and he did not disappoint me.

I learnt not too long ago from his wife, who I didn't see for quite a long time, after asking about his health, that he had passed away, being diabetic. It really hit me like a ton of bricks, getting that news. All I can truly say is he was a good soldier to me and I will never forget what he did for me. I know he lived his life his way and God was ready to take him when he did. May his soul rest in peace. And for all the people that he would have helped just like me, I say a hearty thank you, and from all of us who are still alive, I dedicate this chapter to Mr. Kisson. I would also draft him into our hall as one of the pillars of our new town.

Stumpy's Emporium; home to many small businesses.

We also have another entrepreneurial complex just about 200 meters east of Penny Savers, West City, called Stumpy's Emporium. *Stumpy* is the nickname of Fitzroy Phillips of the Plymouth and Scarborough Phillips. His business was located at Scarborough till he suddenly found out that

Canaan is where he should be and he came and he built, something similar to what Ms. Mabel started. He is into household items, he also has other stores at his establishment, like a one-stop shop. All of these new stores make it much easier, for comfortable and convenient shopping in Canaan/Bon Accord and positively contribute to making our town much more of a congenial atmosphere for everyone.

Going nearer to Crown Point we have Spence's Colosseum, like I said before, just across from where John Grant's Golden Star was situated. He also has several other restaurants occupying his establishment. There is also the Division of Settlements office, an arm of the THA (Tobago House of Assembly), and another pharmacy just opposite.

Some of the businesses located along "the Strip" at Crown Point

There are several restaurants in this vicinity, all types of food and beverages can be had at any time of day or night. Going in the airport's direction from there one can find casinos on the right side of the street, guesthouses and bars. On the left side of the street there are more bars and more shops and a Republic Bank building, and a little further one can find the Coco Reef Hotel, winners of so many prestigious awards in the hotel business. And among all these buildings we have the arm of the law in the Crown Point Police station just adjacent to the A. N.R. Robinson Airport.

Sports, Culture, Education and Religion

Chapter Twenty-Five

There is an institution I think worth mentioning right here, right now. It has to do with our pastime of goat racing. I reserve the right to bring it up because it is a part of Canaan's culture taken up by a special selection of guys namely Winston "Man Baby" Skeete, Wilbert "Scaly" Moses of Canaan and the Potts brothers of Bon Accord, there used to be two other stalwarts in the late Mr. Colbert Joseph, and the late Mr. Peter May Potts, who recently passed on to the great beyond. They dedicated their lives to the sport by breeding and training their animals to run at the goat races wherever and whenever they were called upon.

On another note, there is always talk about where the first goat and donkey races took place on this island, I was assured by a senior citizen of Canaan that the answer to the question is a close toss-up between Mr. Calvin Chapman of the Four roads Bon Accord and Mr. Boatman Roberts of Robert Street Canaan, it is unclear which of them had it first, but there were those races in our village.

The roads were not paved at the time of these early races, so the running was not hard on those animals' feet. Every year there were donkey and goat races in front of Calvin's shop at Easter time. I'm not sure of the timing of the goat races at Boatman's but there were walking races and long distance running from Scarborough to Canaan during the Easter sports meetings in Canaan.

Mt. Pleasant and Buccoo came long after we showed them how it should be done. Nowadays they have goat races at

Top; exterior of the Buccoo Integrated Facility. Bottom the interior of the Buccoo Integrated Facility showing the field, tracks and starting gates for the running of the goat races.

least four times a year since the inception of the new Buccoo facilities.

I always wonder if it is worth it, the time it takes to take the goats to the sea to swim to strengthen their legs and build stamina, it is hard work. I also found out that goats can start racing as young as one year old and can race until they are ten years old, and let's not forget how sweet the meat can be. Just like horses, they need special care, feed and practice sessions. Then finding the right jockey to race the goats takes another painstaking effort.

These guys really must have had a great love for the sport to invest so much of their time and energy. They are very dedicated to their goats.

The Canaan interest in goat races has been here for a while even though the races are a few times a year the community still shows up ready for the races. The Tobago House of Assembly (THA) has built a special track at Buccoo for those goats complete with starting gates just like for horses.

At first, I thought of it as a tourist attraction, but it seems to have blossomed into something more. I guess it is what it is. They must be getting some reward to invest in those goats otherwise they would have dropped them a long time ago.

I can only see it as being done for the competitive spirit attached to the sport, and that camaraderie that emanates through the goats' owners that keeps that flag flying as high as it does. I also think it's a feather in Tobago's cap to be the only country in the world to have goat races. We are fortunate to have the goats' owners investing in taking it to another level. I think they should have punters with odds on placed bets just like horse races. And with the technology of today it should encourage online betting to move with the times in which we live. I dedicate this chapter exclusively to all the goat owners and trainers who kept the art of goat racing alive and well throughout the years, taking into consideration the longevity of the sport. I'm in my seventies and goat racing was here before I was even born, so something must be said to show the publics' appreciation to the family of goat owners throughout our island.

It is sort of patriotic the way that the evolution of goat racing has survived all the turmoil over the years before those real starting gates were introduced and the course at Buccoo was built.

I can clearly remember being at Mt. Pleasant at Easter anticipating the goats racing down the track, but without the gates it took forever. To get the goats in line to race Because they are not being ridden. Also the length of the rope has to be shortened by the jockey so the goat can be in check for the start, but after the start the specific full length of the rope is used. At that time flags were the starting symbol, but with the introduction of the gates all of that time wasting disappeared, causing the entire crowd to heave a collective sigh of relief.

I do applaud and show my complete respect and admiration to the goat racing community for their effortless endearing contribution to the sport and wish them longevity and fruitful rewards throughout the rest of their career because the whole community keeps looking forward to spending happy afternoons frolicking with their friends and family while enjoying the sport that they made possible with their dedication. Kudos go out to each and every one of those goat owners.

I make special mention of Mr. Winston "Man Baby" Skeete, a veteran of the races. He was fortunate to be given his first goat by a good friend at a very young age. He named it *Please Yourself*, and it did please him very much.

I was told that he became an owner just by luck; two kids were born to the mother whose name was Fire Queen, a retired racing goat. The owner was so disheartened to have one of the kids killed by a car he decided to give away the other kid and "Man Baby" was the lucky recipient. That kid turned out to be such a wonderful gift by winning several races and trophies, putting Man Baby's name into goat racing history. Kudos must be given to Mr. Geddes Bristol also for being such a good jockey. It's such a strange story because he bought another goat and named it Tourist attraction, but it wasn't worth the price, hence the saying that *"the best things in life are free"* comes to mind.

In case you are wondering, apart from the camaraderie they race for and the bragging rights, there is usually sponsorships for each race so the winner receives that sponsors' trophy. Then there is the winners champion race where all the winners of the day compete in this last race to prove the champion of champions. I was reliably informed that Please Yourself won it quite a few times, the last being 2019. I must thank Mr. Skeete for his selfless dedication to the sport of goat racing on our small island. He has been in

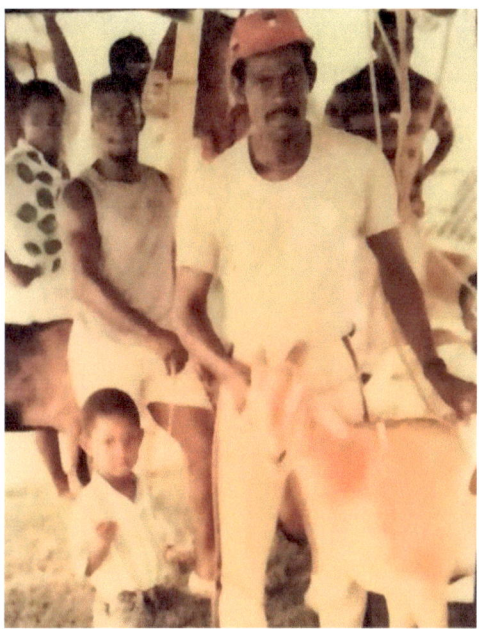

Winston "Man Baby" Skeete getting ready for a race with his favorite goat "Please Yourself"

it for the last 55 years. A sporting pillar without even realizing it.

Goats and their jockeys competing in a race at the Bucco Integrated Facility.

Chapter Twenty-Six

The other side of the sporting spectrum in our village was cricket, in the form of Starlight Cricket Club, which I was told started in 1945. I was not able to get the identities of the foundation members, the best I got was a *"watered-down"* version. They were just remembered as *"Starlight Players"*, with the likes of Adolphus James, Ramon Benjamin, Bobsy Thomas, Israel Williams, John Thomas and his brother Justin, Gareth Hackett, Daniel "Tokyo" Quamina, Errol "Mansom" Kerr, Joseph "Shell" Benjamin, Johnathan "Bat" Thomas, Claudie Williams, the best wicket keeper I ever saw in action and Ignacius "Iggy" Sandy, the best one-handed batsman I ever saw.

I think I should explain about Ignacius Sandy. earlier I said he was a one-handed batsman. Well Iggy, as he was fondly called, was born without all his fingers on one hand and the hand was not fully developed, so he would just have the hand on top of the bat, to sort of help steer the ball to what part of the field he preferred, and steer them he did. He was a troublesome batsman to get out, and not a bad spin bowler too.

In the annals of Tobago cricket, the biggest story was a friendly cricket match that took place at Shaw Park, Tobago, between a cricket side including one of the three Ws. They were all three knighted by the Queen, they were Sir Frank Mortimer Maglinne Worrel, Sir Clyde Leopold Walcott and Sir Everton DeCourcy Weekes. Sir Frank Worrel, who at the time was the captain of the West Indies cricket team, came here for an exhibition game against the *"cream of the crop"* of Tobago cricketers, after all they would be playing against some of the best in the West Indies, including of course the knighted emperor of cricket, Sir Frank M. M. Worrel, who by the way, was forty-two years old when he died, he died of leukemia.

We love cricket here, we have our greats, and Trinidadians love some cricket too. So, it was Shaw Park or you were not alive as a cricket lover.

The scene was like this in Tobago; the Park was sold out, hotels were filled to capacity, rental cars rented out for that weekend. Airplane bookings were a mess, no space was available on the ferries, in those days the ferries were "The Bird of Paradise" and "The Scarlet Ibis". Cars were parked way down by the Lambeau Anglican school from Shaw Park, the closest they could get to watch the game, just imagine having to park one mile away to watch a cricket match. Patrons found seats on the scoreboard, on fences, anywhere they could get a vantage point to see everything. The hucksters were ready with their salt and fresh nuts and their snow-cones.

The match was about to start, it was a lovely day for cricket; the sun was out in all its glory, with blue skies above and a gentle breeze coming in from the sea. The home team won the toss and decided to send in the visitors to bat. The opening batsmen were on the pitch, taking their marks, the crowd roared with the wonderful news, the umpires surveyed the field, checking the players and taking up their positions. The umpire behind the stumps looked back at the bowler, I guess to see which side of the wicket he had chosen to run on, he has chosen over wicket, so the umpire waved his left hand forward to indicate the start of the game and the bowler started his approach. The bowler was Tobago's best, of course, Israel Williams. His run up was about fifteen or twenty yards, true pacer he was. The first ball was a little on the wide side, he might have been a little nervous, or maybe too anxious, but he collected the ball and started his run up again. He was on target and the batsman had to play a defensive stroke. His first over was done and this went on for a few more overs without many runs or wickets.

A wicket was taken, and the anticipation was about to end, what everybody was waiting for, was about to happen. Sir Frank walked to the wicket swinging his bat with his right hand over his head and loosening up his hips swinging his upper torso from left to right. He took his guard and he was ready for anything they threw at him, after all he was knighted for this. He was right-handed.

The first ball from Israel beat him through bat and pad, the cat and mouse game went on for a couple more overs. What was happening was he was being measured for a fitting like a tailor would his client. Israel started his run up and let loose an old fashioned yorker and Sir Frank was clean bowled, middle stump knocked clean out of the ground by *"ah we bwoy"* Mr. Israel Williams. Shaw Park was in awe; can you just take some time to put this into perspective?

The king of cricket, knighted as he was, to come to one of the smallest islands in the world to be bowled out by a son of that soil? It bogles the mind, like David did to Goliath with his sling and a small stone, so in order to save the day the umpire put up his hand for a no ball, the whole of Shaw Park breathed a collective sigh of relief, and Israel finished his over and went into the outfield. Sir Frank went on to make a healthy score to the delight of all assembled, making his strokes to every corner of the ground. That was a match nobody leaving Shaw Park that day, would ever forget,

After the match nobody was interested in the result, all everybody was saying is how Israel was world class to bowl Sir Frank Worrell. But the most important thing coming out of that match that day was Sir Frank knew it wasn't a no ball, he was most definitely beaten with that ball. And he knew everybody knew the truth so in order to appease his conscience he sought out Israel and offered him a place on the West Indies team which Israel declined.

To make matters worse when the media confronted the umpire who made the no ball call, he asked not to be quoted, and with that assurance, he explained that Shaw Park was not filled to see Israel Willams clean bowl Sir Frank Worrell, they were there to see Sir Frank Worrell bat, after all, who was Israel Williams? Nobody ever heard of him, in contrast, every cricket lover, when the West Indies played Australia, would stay up all night just to see Sir Frank Worrell make his strokes.

I must add though, Israel did not bowl on that match after that incident, would you? Israel Williams has passed on to meet his Maker and is sheltered under the wings of His love, may the good Lord bless and keep him in His good graces. This pillar of sports was also our hero.

Chapter Twenty-Seven

Another stalwart of our village was Mr. Lincoln Bobb, he was born to ride a bicycle, a gift inherited from his father Mr. Moses Bobb, who was one of the first cyclists to come out of Canaan. Lincoln grew up having a love for riding on box carts. They were used for fetching water from the nearest standpipe. But the nagging love for a bicycle was always there. He attained the necessary funds for his first bike at twenty years old, when bought, he joined the other guys around who had their bikes and were interested in forming a bike club.

The club was unofficially formed and the other members were Franklyn James, Ellis Peters, and Steve Wilson, with their coach being Mr. Brent Hart. The thing was, because his dad was killed while riding his bike when he was just two years old, which he was not even aware of until then, his mother was totally against his idea until he convinced her that he would be careful. She eventually consented. He had a fulfilling first year and the die was cast, his dream was coming through. He went directly to top cyclist for the first eleven years, winning races at Packer Rebel sports meeting, then Mt. Pleasant Goat races at Easter, at Goodwood Village Council meet, and he competed at the Arima Velodrome, Queens Park Oval, Skinner Park, and Guaracara Park, where he won some races and placed second and third in his category.

He decided to try the road races, in both Trinidad and Tobago where his best was fifth in the Tobago Classic, because of a flat tire and not having the required swift attention he should have had.

His competition in those days were the Farrell brothers and the great Gene Samuel to name a few. His most memorable race was in Trinidad which started at Riverside Plaza to Sangre Grande through to Gran Bazaar then back to Riverside Plaza. It was one hundred and twenty miles long for the National Championship, there were forty-nine starters and only nine finished, of which he was the ninth. He felt he had reached to heights he never expected to reach and he was a proud man that day.

Coming from humble beginnings, catching crabs for his mother to sell at the market to help upkeep his dream of competing with the bigger boys was all a part of who he wanted to be, and he was a happy man. Then there was a great setback when his coach migrated to Canada and left him exposed to just his experience while competing. He then transitioned to the Ironman Triathlon put on by the Rotary Club of Tobago where he came Seventh in the first year, fourth in the second year, and eventually won it in the final year of the competition.

The Abraham brothers were nobodies while racing with those guys for years, nobody ever knew of them, because they were always in the shadow of Lincoln Bobb and his partners from Canaan. It was fortunate for Emille and his fathers' training motorcycle, that it was after Lincoln Bobb came out of racing his space opened for him to be highlighted. We all could then see the real mettle of the man, hence the saying; "when the cat is away, the mice will play". And as the media became more prominent Emille was recognized as a big deal.

Mr. Lincoln Bobb is still alive today, and I consider myself to be fortunate to have him send me his story, because others would want to know, and hear his side of that story. Mr. Emille Abraham was not prominent when Lincoln was riding, he was in the background only eating up Lincoln's and his friends' proverbial dust. I thank Mr. Bobb for clearing up that important fact for me, people would need to know the stories as they happened, from the horses' mouth, so to speak. As the late comedian; Sprangalang would say: *"It couldn't get any better than this".* So here is our candidate for the next pillar of our community, my hat goes off to Mr. Lincoln Bobb for his contribution to the sporting development of this village.

I also take this opportunity to highlight the fact that there are many more stories like Lincoln's that were buried and forgotten because no one thought of making it possible for any of the future generation to have an idea of who and what went before them.

For me, to have knowledge of the past accomplishments of people, especially athletes, could assist in developing new talents. To me, highlighting accounts for posterity is important.

Chapter Twenty-Eight

Somerset Football Club was born around the year nineteen sixty-three with core members, the late Mr. Mervyn "Town Scraper" Garcia and Mr. Hubert Alexis, who were affiliated to Reeves Louis' shop. After half day on Thursday afternoons, they would assemble at the recreation ground for meetings to encourage the youths to form the club.

Eventually, the club was formed and used the Bon Accord recreation ground as their home base but was rudely interrupted by a lady called Flora in September that year. After hurricane Flora the team practiced in the Bon Accord primary school yard because the recreation ground was overrun with tents for villagers who had lost their homes.

And after the tents were removed the recreation ground was not put back there, the Ministry for Tobago Affairs confiscated it and turned it into the new housing area that exists today, The Milford Court.

The Bon Accord Recreation Grounds (2024)

Their first taste of competition was the Tobago Soft Shoe competition, which was run at Shaw Park's two football grounds. The criteria for the competition was the footwear, which had to be any soft shoe, i.e sneakers, gym boots or anything made of canvass, as long as there was no leather material in the shoe. The early Somerset version won it after two years in nineteen sixty-five. Those were hard times in those days and most of the players would mostly practice bare footed, to save their nice soft shoes, until game day when they would put them on.

Some of the players on that team were: Prescot Sandy, Ainsley Woods, Norbert *"Duck Mouth"* Clarke, Linford *"Jingo"* Elliot, Hubert Alexis, Comby, Eudel *"TB"* Cruickshank, Edgar *"Goff"* Trim, Rupert *"Rupee"* Franklyn, Pernell Thomas, Melville *"Mello"* Thomas, Kenlis Dillon, Dennis *"Big Belly"* Roberts. Elgin Ranjitsingh and Ted Quamina were mostly on the bench.

After the 1965 victory there was no more success for a while, which could have been due to the transition to the senior "Hard Shoe" competition and the coming aboard of Somerset's first coach in none other than Mr. Winfield Quamina.

There is a selfless story about one of the members. Denis *"Big Belly"* Roberts owned the football, and because of it felt he should play every game whether he practiced or not. So, to get out of that predicament another player paid two years subscription in advance so the club could buy their own football. That other player was none other than Melville *"Mello"* Thomas. The things some people do to create a peaceful atmosphere, I do commend *"Mello"*. A new football with laces at that time was just about $8.95, and the upgraded version without laces went up to $13.75.

We have lost a lot of our past players, they have gone to the great beyond, but I can at least give you an idea of some of the history they proudly left behind.

I think special note should be granted to our goalkeeper, none other than Mr. Prescot *"Preco"* Sandy, He dazzled between those uprights, when shots went to him it just seemed that he was always in his element and the confidence he gave us as outfield players had no equal. I could clearly remember seeing him change direction in midair because the shot was deflected off a player, *Preco* always made the save. May the good Lord Bless his soul and keep him under his wings of love for eternity.

A few of the others who left their indelible mark on the sport of football were one of our first captains; Boysie *"Man Shoe"* Mitchell, who was a stalwart in defense. Then we had George *"Cacho"* Archer, one of the sweetest left footed midfielders I ever saw, then there was Kenlis Dillon playing on my left, an inside left I could depend on. We also had Joseph *"Shell"* Benjamin, Pernell Thomas, Harrison *"Bing"* Cox, Leslie *"Castle Poona"* Moses, Elgin Ranjitsingh, Norbert *"Duck Mouth"* Clarke, Ephraim *"Tokes"* Dearie, Lloyd Thornhill, Dennis and his brother Ainsley Woods, Ian and his brother Boysie Cruickshank, Combi, Ted Quamina, may the good Lord shelter all my deceased teammates under His wings of love, they are surely missed.

There are some of us who are still alive and who need commendation too such as; Leroy *"Brisso"* Bristol who was my dependable right winger bringing me those crosses as often as he did. I was his inside right, he made one of those crosses unintentionally knock out a defender named Chris,

Front row left to right: Augustus "Doc" Mitchell (holding the Tobago Football Association Sheild), Orman "Voon" Forde, Samuel "Cutcake" Benjamin, Horace "Tozie" Alfred, Pernell Thomas, Pedro Hernandez, and Lennox "Little Ting" Quamina. Back row: right to left George "Catcho" Archer, Boysie "Gango" Waldron, Leroy " Brisso" Bristol, Rupert "Rupee" Franklin, Lloyd "Chupid"Thornhill, Edgar"Goff"Trim and Eudel "TB" Cruickshank.

he was a defender on the opposing team, putting himself at risk in defense. He found out that day the power of the man making those crosses and by extension tasted some of what I controlled and scored in all of those games.

Then the maestro in the midfield Rupert "Rupee" Franklyn, another of our *"dependables"*, Rupee playing alongside Cacho was like a battalion charging forward saying get out of the way, the heart of Somerset is coming at you. Then we had Terry Williams, Vallier George, Linford *"Jingo"* Elliot, Eudel *"TB"* Cruickshank, Gareth Hackett and James *"Jum"* Roberts. Our other goalkeepers Francis Henry and Michael Cox, Lennox *"Lil Thing"* Quamina, Melville *"Mello"* Thomas was skinny only in stature off the field, on it, he was one to reckon with. Hubert Alexis, Boysie *"Gango"* Waldron, Curtis *"Half Day"* John, Theophilus Trim, Carlston Gray, Chris James, Augustus *"Doc"* Mitchell, Leslie *"Papers"* Waithe, Fitzherbert *"Soomby"* Roberts, and Ezekiel "Ram" Benjamin.

So now I will venture further to remind everyone of the guys of what they accomplished while playing on one of the best football teams in Tobago. For the Soft Shoe Competition of 1965 Boysie Waldron, scored all three goals to beat Youth Camp 3-0 for Somerset's first League Trophy. Then in 1966 Somerset won their second competition beating Wanderers 1-0 to take home the Federal Tobacco Trophy. In 1967 Somerset won the Solo Cup. In 1970 that Somerset won The League Shield, the Solo Cup and the Ragbir Trophy. I think we can all pat ourselves on our backs for a job well done leaving a legacy like that is tremendous for our village, and for that I say job well done to all the team. We had one more notable triumph in 1972 when we beat Wanderers 2-1 at the new Mt. Pleasant recreation ground with Patience Hill's sensational star, and with notable National player Ralph *"Arab"* Nelson in attendance, it was the talk of the town.

I cannot in good conscience leave this segment on Somerset football throughout its coming to life and becoming defunct without showing my gratitude and total appreciation to the one person, one of the foundation members of Somerset, and one of our most modest stars. I am talking about none other than Mr. George Rupert Franklyn, who we all know as Rupee. He confided in me that George is his first name and how he got it, that's for another story. His memory is phenomenal, and I mean that with every fiber of my being, this man's memory goes back as far as his first day in Somerset and before, he remembers the games and who scored or was booked, the names of all the trophies we won, what year, and how we celebrated. He is just amazing and kudos go out to him for his memory, I have a special wish that he has a long productive life so anytime any flashback is needed he will be around for us to ask him to help us out. Another example of one of our pillars.

Chapter Twenty-Nine

I would like to delve into a sport that I love, to show the appreciation to a set of Athletes who I think excelled in their particular field of expertise, and I might even venture to say as a Tobagonian that being branded as such was a curse after all the hoorah was quieted down. The powers that be would make like they would be showing solidarity for those athletes, pretending to back them all the way but just praying for the hoorah to die down so they can breathe a welcomed sigh, of more than welcome relief.

Tobagonians have been treated like aliens ever since I can remember in every field of life, and a perfect example is a story which came to forefront in the late 1980s. Most people would not want to revisit this episode, but this writer is of the firm belief that this is the perfect forum to reconstruct that story, and mind you, every word is just as it happened.

This young schoolboy of Canaan, I won't have to call any name, but the world knows the story from bits and pieces. I can assure you that I could put the bits with the pieces because this young man was at my home almost every day, eating, drinking, watching television, and playing table tennis.

During the afternoon hours, after his school day was through, he would head to the recreation ground where he honed his skill as the new football talent found in Tobago. The high school football competition was won by the Signal Hill Comprehensive school that year because of the emerging skill of that young man. You can just imagine, coming from that small village in Tobago it might have seemed like he was carrying the whole of Tobago on his young shoulders, and not even eighteen years old yet, but I think he carried it well.

Because of his skill throughout that competition, he was noticed by the football elite in Trinidad and the story really begins. The young man had a troubled youth, is all I would say, but his skill was magical. I must ask to be excused for the use of that word because it was given to another footballer of Trinidadian heritage right around the same time, and you might not want to imagine how the football landscape was about to make a drastic change because of it. To me and a whole lot of others, especially Tobagonians, were not as impressed with that little magician as we were with *"ah we own bwoy"* so it was like a competition between the two of them. Asking me, I would have said the right name was given to the wrong player.

An international match came up and our boy was called to practice for the game, there were challenges that he had to overcome to travel and stay in Trinidad, unknown by the coaching staff and others involved in their preparations. Anyway, match day came and that's when the things started to happen.

It was a toss-up when to bring on *"ah we bwoy"* in the game, but the *"Lil Magician"* played right through. He was Trinidadian and his people were coming to see him play. You could put your pot on the fire he would play the whole game. Nobody knew how the Tobago boy got the funding to travel to Trinidad except the Cassa from that recreation club in Canaan.

The Cassa would tax the games and put funds aside for his travelling expenses and board, he had to eat too, for the time he was in Trinidad for the game. Even if it was for ten minutes of game time, he had to stay the weekend. Most times that ten minutes was all he got. The Cassa never complained about the responsibility, they were neighbors, and he knew the young man's situation and he made a vow to help him anyway he could, and he did, right up until Aston Villa F.C. signed him and took him to Bermingham, England.

I admire the selflessness of the Cassa in this undertaking of love and devotion to that young man, and just to see how he turned out with his huge contract, everyone would think all was well there that ends well. Think again. It hurts me to say that he left the Cassa out in the cold after it all. The fame got to his head big time, that's where I think God paid him with his first son. One must never damn the bridge one has crossed.

Coming up to World Cup elimination time late 1980s, the same thing applied, a few minutes of game time and that was it, but he persevered, and the Trinidad and Tobago team qualified as the smallest country to ever qualify for any World Cup that year. That was when things started to happen for *"ah wee bwoy"*, the world was watching all the performances and the same people who watched the *Lil Magician* watched our boy too. The time came for the powers that be to make their choices among the stars of the World Cup and lo and behold they both caught the eyes of scouts, *Lil Magician* got chosen for Glasgow Rangers in Scotland, then went to Hibernian F.C. while our boy was chosen by a Team in the E.P.L. (English Premier League) arguably one of the best leagues in the world, to Aston Villa, where he played 284 games and scored 97 goals, after a few years later he transferred to one of the biggest teams in the world of football, I'm talking about Manchester United with Sir Alex Ferguson, the best coach in the world at the time, partnering Mr. Andy Cole in 152 appearances he scored 65 goals and helped to win the treble his second year with the club. The only thing though is how he treated the people who helped him to get where he did, old people would say, *"like a fowl, after he done eat he belly full, he wipe he mouth on the ground, and he forget".* Apart from all that reader, could you tell me who was the better player in your honest opinion? That question's answer again would depend on who is answering whether it's a Trinidadian or a Tobagonian. That's the way it has been all our lives, we must settle for the crumbs from their Trinidad table.

Chapter Thirty

I want to change gears here a bit by mentioning one of our track stars in none other than the late Mr. Desmond Victor Emmanuel Melville, known to all as *"Dezo"*, who was born on fifth February 1946. He became a Fire Officer in later years but I mostly remember him as a footballer first and foremost, playing with us at the old recreation grounds before hurricane Flora, and after it in the schoolyard of Bon Accord Primary School.

I can clearly recall an incident on the school grounds. One day when playing football, the ball was passed to *"Dezo"* on the right wing and while moving forward to get to that byline before he crossed it to me to take my shot, his foot collided with some stones that were imbedded in the ground with just the top above the ground. *"Dezo"* had not remembered the exact spot, we all knew the stones were there and had been playing around them for quite a while. But this day was not *"Dezo's"* because he made his cross just at the top of those stones and the sound it made resonates in my ear even today, bringing back the memory of the sight of the top of his toes.

Everyone knew what to expect as he felt the pain and fell to the ground, uttering a sound that was so cold as he held his foot. We all ran over to him and watched the white of his foot slowly turn to red as the blood started to flow over the top of all his five toes. That memory stayed with me for quite a long time and I still remember it today. We offered assistance because in those days nobody went to the hospital for a small thing like that, not to spend the rest of

Right; Desmond Melville (Dezo) competing in a race.

the week there, so he got up and went home to lick his wound, so to speak.

All of that happened before his athletic career took off. He became a national athlete representing Trinidad and Tobago in the 400 meters and the 800 meters during the latter part of the sixties and early seventies. And because of his prowess in his athletic field, he was granted an athletic scholarship to attend Grambling State University, Louisiana in the USA in 1973. He went further to be chosen as a member of the All-American College Track and field team of the year 1974. He concluded his scholarship at the university and graduated with a Bachelor of Arts and Sciences Degree in 1976.

Having completed his studies in the USA, he returned to Trinidad and Tobago and went into teaching at Northeastern College, Sangre Grande in 1977, until he was transferred to

Roxborough Composite School at Roxborough, Tobago in 1979.

As a teacher he continued to contribute to the development of local athletes here in Tobago, helping them to obtain numerous national championships and assisting them in obtaining international scholarships for several local athletes.

Desmond Victor Emmanuel Melville, better known as *"Dezo",* passed away in 2002, he was 56 years old, leaving to mourn his wife Cynthia Walcott Melville, and four children Jaiye, Darnell, Akil, and Cuquie.

In retrospect, *"Dezo"* in his relatively short existence hit all the high notes that came his way, including beating some of the best 400m and 800m athletes who were around in Trinidad at the time, that pleases me so much, because of the facilities the people in power in sports provide for us here in Tobago. There was no Dwight Yorke stadium in Tobago at that time, most of these athletes' main track away from the schoolyards and traces was the beach, having been blessed with raw talent.

I usually say to my counterparts, I live in "Trinidad but Tobago", because I feel like an alien from a different country or planet, because that is how we are being treated locally. So, when one of us rises above their quality and can produce the goods they feel intimidated after looking at what we used to become better than they are, as Trinbagonian.

I thank you *"Dezo",* for giving me and many others like me, who gloried in your spirit something to hold on to, because of all you achieved in your sporting career. And though you are no longer here, we all know you did it your way, lived your life to its fullest. We remember you by your successes and you will always be a pillar to our youths who are looking for someone to pattern their young lives after. I hereby declare you as officially another pillar of Canaan, Bon Accord and Crown Point. Fifty-six years, it was short, but it was sweet.

Bottom left Desmond Melville (Dezo) sitting with teammates

Chapter Thirty-One

Keeping with the sport of running this one might shock you; Mr. Haseley Crawford was our first Olympic gold medalist, for that I take my hat off to the man. But have a conversation with him and he will tell you that there were two guys from Tobago, Mr. Fitzherbert *"Soombie"* Roberts and Mr. Kenaul Shaw who beat him at Southern Games before the Canadian Olympics, at his favorite distance, the one hundred meters. It encourages me now to indicate the attitude of the Trinidadians who paid no mind to those two guys who beat Crawford, who, by the way, were not affiliated with any club, it was just pure Tobago talent.

We, meaning Trinidad and Tobago, could have had three finalists in that 100 meters final in Canada in 1976, and could have come away with three medals. Female Jamaican sprinters did it. But having beaten their boy at Southern Games into third place they simply decided to go with Crawford and chance a medal than take Shaw and Roberts and have their boy lose a chance at that gold. Trinidadians never looked at having Gold, Silver and Bronze because Crawford's chances would have been at best, bronze. So, it was like the Tobago boys never happened and their win was pushed so far under the carpet that the longest broom couldn't get to it. And the reason for that? They were from Tobago.

Oh, those two guys are still alive today so if it sounds unbelievable just take a trip to Tobago. I'll be your host to find them to confirm the authenticity of my story.

I can also boast that if anyone knows Mr. Rawle Swanston, if they can find him sober, they can ask him how he got his four-year scholarship to university in the USA. I can give you my story, Rawle and I went to school together at Hillview College El Dorado Road, Tunapuna, next to a playing field with a track and a cricket pitch in the middle, called Honeymoon. I beat him in the one hundred meters and two hundred meters, I was 15 years old and fast, no athletic club affiliation either. There were pictured finishes of our races up on our school notice board a couple days after, showing him being dethroned, grimacing while leaning at the tape, in his loss. The king of the track no more, to a never heard of Ken Gordon, your humble servant, then he invited me to join Burnley Athletics Club at St. Augustine, which I did. Those were the days of Thora Best and Millicent Cumberbatch, both from Tunapuna. And I can remember also Edwin Skinner and Anthony Spencer were track athletes too during that same period.

Burnley's Coach was Mr. George N. Clarke, he walked with a limp, and he rode his bike to practice sessions. Rawle Swanston never beat me and after beating him along with the cream of the crop from the rest of the Caribbean at Eastern Games at Walker Park, somewhere in Central Trinidad, I had a conversation with Clarkie, my coach, about a scholarship, but he told me that because of my academics, he was unable to assist me in anyway. It broke my heart, I did love beating people, those boasting Trinidadians, especially Rawle, knowing he was behind me all the time trying his very best, after every race he found out his strategy failed another time, and his best was not good enough. So being an understanding guy I just hung up my track shoes then and there, it was then early 1963.

The next four-year scholarship opening was given to Mr. Rawle Swanston, with no thank you of course, when the cat is away it's time for the rat to play, and I never blamed him, it was his, and I could not go anywhere near it. I think whatever is for someone no one else can ever have it. In summation of this episode, I had the opportunity to have a chance encounter with Rawle, sometime before Covid, at Queens Park Savannah, and he was in a really bad shape, we talked, but mostly incoherently on his part. It was not pretty, from his attire to his demeanor, I could think of one word to describe him properly, and the word I came up with was "sad",

Ken Gordon holding trophy for Sportsman of the Years 1959-1963.

although he was supposed to be some kind of engineer. To see a brother in that state, no matter what the situation, could never make me feel good, the bottom line was he needed help bad. Could someone please look him up and see if you can help him, he was my schoolmate and friend.

The next time I ever won anything from running was at a sports meeting at Bon Accord Recreation ground, it was a Pyrex dish, I still have it today, from sometime in the 1970s. I was blessed with talent, and I took up football thereafter and didn't do too badly, because I made the Somerset team and scored a few goals. I had a nice career playing an attacking inside right or left, as the team required, and scored with both feet too. I was their penalty taker as a number nine.

I am very proud that right now as I write I have a grandson who was born in the UK who was chosen by a Chelsea scout for training with that club all of August this year 2024. To top it all off I still have my Somerset football socks, in great condition too, from the 1970s, which I will make as a gift to him handing down the rest of my talent into his care. I want to be there for every day of his training, hopefully with God's help I can see him play, it will surely be a blessing. I get goose bumps just thinking about him playing football at that level.

Chapter Thirty-Two

Another sore point I'll bring up, since I've known politics in this country, we have had two Sports Ministers of Tobago heritage, spanning over four decades, and neither one ever took the time to notice that there has never been an indoor complex in Tobago, up to today in 2024, with the second one presently in office. This reference to sports ministers is totally in keeping with how it relates to athletes from my village. The whole world needs to know how we cope with unfair treatment.

They get in their chauffeur driven limousines and travel the length and breadth of Trinidad to open brand spanking new indoor complexes, some communities even have more than one, scissors in hand to cut ribbons to cherished applauses.

Then they fly home to Tobago and smile with their constituents showing them how much they love and care for them because they see them around their community, maybe walking for exercise, come election they say: *"Ah ah we gyal who else ah we guh put, yuh nuh see she ah wark thru de village?"* Even though while walking through the village she never says good morning or good evening to anyone, not even senior citizens like me, she just looks me straight in my eyes and passes on by. No respect or what old people call good manners and no broughtupsy. I heard recently that she got put in her place in a public setting by her boss.

This is no joke, I took my daughter to Shaw Park, one afternoon for an evening of me watching basketball while she was watching netball, it was a disaster. On the asphalt there were white lines drawn for the netball court just inches away from the white lines drawn for the basketball court.

The problem began as both games were playing at the same time; any time there was an infringement and the referee had to blow the whistle there was confusion. If the foul happened on the netball court and the whistle blew the basketball game would stop, nobody could say which court had an infringement. I just looked at my daughter, and she knew it was time to go because how could one enjoy a game like that? And this is the year 2024. There is still not one indoor complex in Tobago, to play these games in comfort.

Google just told me that there are 19 indoor complexes in Trinidad and Tobago, I'll name every one of them and you check for yourself to see how many are in Tobago. 1: Jean Pierre Sports Complex, Port of Spain, 2:National Racquet Sport Center, Tacarigua, 3: La Joya Sporting Complex, St Joseph, 4:Eastern Regional Indoor Sport Arena, Tacarigua, 5:Central Regional Indoor Sport Arena(Chaguanas Sporting Complex) Chaguanas, 6:Ultimate Indoor facility, San Juan, 7: Mayaro Sport Facility, Mayaro, 8: Eastern Regional Sporting Complex, Tacarigua, 9:Petrotrin Clifton Hill Sports Grounds, Point Fortin, 10: Irwin Park, Siparia, 11: Arima Velodrome, Arima, 12: North Eastern Regional Multipurpose Sport Facility, Sangre Grande, 13: Mahaica Oval, Point Fortin, 14: Diego Martin Sporting Complex, Diego Martin15:North Eastern sporting Complex, 16:UWI Sports and physical Education Centre, St. Augustine, 17: Fatima College Pavilion, Port of Spain, 18: Barataria Ball Players Cricket oval, San Juan, 19: Republic Bank Sports

Complex, San Juan. OUT OF 19, NOT ONE IS IN TOBAGO, but internationally, the complexes are within Trinidad and Tobago, fake/false news. But the thing is if anyone tells the Tobagonian Sports Minister this information, I doubt it very much if she would even look it up to verify it for authenticity. I'm forced to say again, **"the pen is mightier than the sword,"** so let us see how true this statement is.

That's not all there is to it, when we send someone down there who possess the skill that is not available in Trinidad, I guess because we here are not being afforded the necessary facilities it is surprising the skill we nurture, so they must go through hoops to outshine or out class anything they have close in quality of talent there.

We are not aliens or Grenadians/Bajans/Guyanese here, it's supposed to be one nation. We are the other half of what are called Trinbagonians, please say it slowly so it can resonate and stick. Imagine if we had a couple of those 19 complexes, just two, the talent we would turn out, our flag is in the same colors as yours. We didn't beg anyone to join this other half of the country. We were unified in 1889, that is over 135 years ago, but we are still seeking the unity today we were supposed to have gained since then. We are still being treated like an *"outside child",* better known as a bastard or maybe an *"unwanted stepchild".* Anyone representing Tobago automatically represents Trinidad, but we must be of a higher caliber than a compatriot from Trinidad to be even considered to get an opportunity for a trial period.

It's a ridiculous scenario but that's still the way it is today. That discriminatory habit must end. As I said before, *enough is enough*, we are out of other cheeks to turn, it reminds me of our THA (Tobago House of Assembly) fighting for the recognition it deserves when asking for a piece of the pie every year at budget time to run things for Tobago. If that's not discrimination, then I must go back to school to find out the proper definition of the word. I was deprived of a full education, and I left school before the word came up, my bad! Don't misunderstand me though, I never cry over spilt milk, never. I think I did good for myself so far. What do you think?

I have said all of that just to highlight what I really want to tell the world of; that is the God given sporting talent we possess here in Tobago. I'll call a few names, which I believe everyone in Trinidad has remembered to forget. There was Ralph *"Arab"* Nelson, Dwight Yorke, Desmond Melville, Rebecca Roberts, Claude Noel, Israel Williams, Lincoln Bobb, Linton Williams, Ramon Desouza, Wayne Stewart, Althea George and Lucille George, Fitzherbert Roberts, Kenaul Shaw and Ken Gordon, most of whom represented Trinidad and Tobago, do any of those names ring any bells? I didn't think so, at least not to any Trinidadians, but they are all well known to all of Tobago. Just to rub it in, and I, Ken G Gordon, beat Mr. Rawle Swanston at 100 meters at Eastern Games before he got his scholarship to a university in the USA.

I do believe that my nation as a whole is comprised of two islands, but from where I sit to take a good look at the arrangements between these two islands, I need much better spectacles than the ones I usually wear, because I'm not seeing the equality. I say this because having lived in

Tobago for most of my life I still feel like we are not fully appreciated as we should be as Trinbagonians. Especially when I look at the sporting facilities that we must use compared to Trinidad. It breaks my heart to see our youths break their backs, trying twice as hard to achieve success and to make the right impression when they must compete with a Trinidadian, who has all the right tools at their disposal to be at their best.

Can anyone imagine how different it is when you are accustomed to bouncing a netball on asphalt, then to have to compete on the correct hard floor for netball and basketball, that puts the Tobago player at a disadvantage right from the start. But do you think the Tobago powers that be, have any knowledge of that comparison? Yes, she does. But the license to bring the scissors to Tobago to cut that special ribbon for an indoor complex cannot be had because the Tobago born Sports Minister just doesn't care about asking for one, a pair of scissors or an Indoor complex. So, it's back to square one every season, whether its Volleyball, Netball or Basketball. What about Gymnastics, Boxing and Martial Arts? How did we find a champion in Claude Noel? He trained in Trinidad, but we all know he is a Tobagonian.

Just like I mentioned before, there's not even one indoor complex on this island, not one, and there are 19 (nineteen) in Trinidad, some communities have more than one, you can Google it. How do you think that makes our athletes feel? I can tell you; they all feel like stepchildren/bastards. Now, no matter what part of the country you live in, that arrangement could never be fair, and unless the Tobago child's potential is more exceptional than his counterpart, he has no chance to shine or make it. And when he does make it, it's like double jeopardy, he is damned if he does and damned if he doesn't. And most times it's not worth the effort.

Another way of solving it is by leaving the country and going abroad to hone their skills and when they are heard about again, they are participating in events under a new flag. Then the Trinidadians get up in arms against them for taking that route. Tobagonians don't think the same way because we know why it had to be done.

All it would take is to give us an equal piece of the proverbial pie. If you cut the ribbon to open one more indoor complex start making plans to open one in Tobago, or as a matter of fact, ask for one now, don't wait until you open another one there, open both the same day, one in Trinidad and then one in Tobago. So, for Trinidad to have all nineteen does anyone see any discrepancy?

To quote from our National Anthem, *"Side by side we stand…. Islands of the blue Caribbean Sea….and it goes on to say…Here, every Creed and Race find an equal place"*. Truth be told, most of us here in Tobago are still trying to find that equal place, and it's not for want of trying since 1962 when we as a country gained independence. As a Tobagonian we are in a handicapped race, but from behind, Trinidad is always in front of us. I speak my mind in calling a spade a spade. Side by side, equality, remember?

Please don't misunderstand me, this is all because of love for my country, and by extension my beautiful Island, and what I would like to see happen for the betterment of the youths of today and tomorrow, allowing them to fulfill their full potential. I have a great grandson now, I'm so happy he's living in Trinidad though, I'll travel to see him, and I'm just thinking about how I could help to make it easier for him and the many others like him who would be in need of modern facilities to practice their craft, whatever it might be.

Sport is a healthy pastime, and should always be encouraged in the youths, because it keeps them off the streets and out of trouble. I think it helps develop responsibility and pride in oneself, which is always good, and for the best.

Chapter Thirty-Three

This story is about one of our female athletes, Ms. Lucille George, of Bon Accord. She was mentored at Western Springfield, as a member from 1970, training from her elementary school days at Bon Accord under Mr. James Trim as her coach for almost four years. In 1974, while at Secondary school she blossomed out to gain her recognition by representing Tobago. That was when she was chosen to wear the national colors of Trinidad and Tobago to compete at those 1974 CARIFTA GAMES at Jamaica where she won a silver medal in the Javelin and Shot Putt. In doing so, she became the FIRST CARIFTA GAMES MEDALIST in her field, representing her country, and her being from Tobago.

Later in that same year she again represented Trinidad and Tobago at the CONCACAF GAMES in Maracaibo, Venezuela but was unsuccessful and disappointed not to be among the medalist. As she would say, she was out of sorts from all the travelling. Anyone can Imagine the highs overcoming all the lows from past years, like breathing a sigh of relief and patting herself on her back and saying she did her best with a degree of satisfaction, there's nothing more anyone could ask of her.

From there she decided to call it a day, but to stay in the game in a different capacity. She became the President of the Western Springfield Sports Club, relieving Ebenezer George to lesser responsibilities. And folks, a gentle reminder that this took place over half a century ago and it took this author's efforts to bring her story to light along with all the others here.

Then there was another young woman from Bon Accord who was instrumental in making some waves on the track as another member of Western Springfield Sports Club. Her name was Ms. Rebecca Roberts. She represented Trinidad and Tobago at the 1977 CARIFTA GAMES in Barbados, where she copped a bronze medal. The following year she also represented Trinidad and Tobago at the 1978 CARIFTA GAMES in Nassau Bahamas and also went to CENTRAL AMERICAN and CARIBBEAN GAMES in Medellin, where she was unfortunate not to medal.

She had a very busy year and I guess it took a toll on her because she also went to the CENTRAL and AMERICAN CHAMPIONSHIPS in Xalapa, Mexico and attended the COMMONWEALTH GAMES in Alberta, Canada. Even as a member of the 4 x 100 relay but there was no more success. However; there were other meetings in Guyana where she got silvers.

I don't want you to misunderstand or underestimate the meaning behind my procuring these achievements from all these athletes. The idea is to showcase what they did for the community they represented. They were all born with their individual talent, and they didn't hide their talents under a bush, if they did, I would have nothing to write about today. And it gives me so much pleasure to write about them here because I was just like them at one time, I have the opportunity to showcase them for the first time along with some of my achievements.

Theirs were mostly in the 1970s but mine were in the 1960s, and only the spectators who were there and still have their faculties intact would be able to recall any of my exploits in my time. As the years go by those people get fewer all the time, but they can be in here for posterity.

Also, if you want to look at it another way, people who read this book can one day hear someone call their name and having read about you can come up to you and still congratulate you on a job well done because they now know of your accomplishments. But what do you think would eventually happen if you never had an opportunity to showcase your work? I can tell you; it fades away and dies a natural death, then nobody will remember your identity or what you accomplished. In the 1950s I helped Bon Accord Elementary school win their first athletics Championship by winning all of my races, the 100, 200and 400 meters long jump and the 4 x 100 relay. A couple of years ago I was told that one of my grandsons was going to school there and in enquiring about him I decided to ask about my athletics records there, just to be told there is none. I really felt let down.

I have to change gears again and move forward to a later time to highlight the athletic career of another young man of our community who excelled on the track in the 1970s, his name is Mr. Linton Williams. He started representing Bon Accord Government Primary school in football, Cricket and athletics but excelled in track. He also represented Tobago schools in Trinidad in the 100m and the 200m in 1972/73 and won both events at 12 years old. He then joined Western Springfield and was coached by Mr. James Trim and Mr. Ebenezer George. He then went on to represent Trinidad and Tobago at the JUNIOR PAN AMERICAN GAMES in Mexico in 1975 where he placed third in the 100m and second in the 200m.

He competed in the senior level in 1979 against Halsey Crawford and came third in the 100m, which earned him a place on the Trinidad and Tobago team for the PANAM GAMES in Puerto Rico where he ran the third leg of the 4x100 with Halsey Crawford and placed fifth.

During that same year he received a scholarship to Seton Hall University where he represented the university at the Melrose Games, Pen relays, and Big East Champions. But his best showing during his college career was winning the 100m and 200m races. He graduated with a degree in finance in 1983. After graduation he continued to compete along with some coaching.

The athletes in my village and in Tobago as a whole got a push to achieve internationally because of one man, Mr. Wilton John of Guy Street, Canaan. Mr. john had the vision for athletes in Tobago, he started a club in the Moravian Church yard at Bon Accord, it was around the year 1969. He, along with Ebenezer "Cuz" George, a young coach at the time saw the vision to build Tobagonian athletes.

It was called Western Springfield Athletic Club with their motto: "Learn to Associate, Compete and Achieve." The club is defunct now, but it was a thriving machine at one time, and I can show where the athletes gave a very good account of themselves.

They started training at our first recreation ground with Cuz, but needed more exclusivity and went into the Bon Accord Government school yard for a little more privacy, some athletes need areas where they can concentrate better on what they are about.

That was the beginning of what turned out to be the making of our new stars, culminating in the National Amateur Athletic Association awarding Mr. Ebenezer George CARIFTA COACH 1975-1980. Cuz, becoming advanced in age, having coached for a little over forty years decided to call it a day in 2010.

Having had the pleasure of seeing the likes of Rebecca Roberts excel at that Carifta Games and Desmond Melville and Linton Williams acquire four-year scholarships abroad at foreign universities as his highest accomplishments. Hats off to a wonderful career, full of sacrifice and dedication, to a humble native of our soil and a true pillar of our community.

Chapter Thirty-Four

Moving from one from sport to entertainment; my love for music began at Hillview College, El Dorado Road, Tunapuna, Trinidad, the fifth school I attended. After leaving school I was seeking my own identity, and without any foundation in any field because of an unjust principal at the sixth school I attended, I struggled to meet the expectations I had for myself.

One night while passing our local pan tent I heard one of my favorite songs being played. I stopped in my tracks, and I listened for a while, it sounded great, I was trapped. I did the only thing available for me then, I sat down. The name of that song was: *"Beautiful Dreamer"*, I found out years later it was sung by Roy Orbison. That's how my steelpan career started.

I went into the pan tent, told the arranger, Mr. Samuel *"Cojar"* Blacks, that I thought I was ready to learn to play any pan available. He said there was a pair of double guitars which needed some lovable attention, and I volunteered my attention to them with "Beautiful Dreamer" being the first song I learnt. I played the double guitars for around five years, until I thought the guitar was too easy to play and transferred my interest to the single tenor pan.

It was a stroke of genius for me later financially, because as a tenor player I had to be in the front line up when performing. Our main performances were done at a reputable hotel twice a week, being in the front made visitors' access to me much easier than the double guitars which were placed in the middle where no one notices that player.

So, as I was playing at the front the visitors would come up to my pan and watch me play the tune and while doing that, they would usually drop a tip in my pan, unnoticed by anyone. That was how I was rewarded for playing music for the first time in my life.

The managers of the band never paid us. The excuses were always about expenditure for the pans and transportation and payments for the arranger, you name it they covered it, but no man playing pan got paid. We got food at the hotel, and Old Oak rum to drink from the sponsors, the sponsors were Fernandes Old Oak Rum. The managers had no other jobs but eventually we saw them buying new cars and living high, putting two and two together I keep getting four, so eventually after eight years I called a spade a spade and I left.

I had no idea I had saved that much money from the tips and I also had a small job washing cars during the day. My dream was to stay with what I loved doing, that was music. I had my hero in the field and his name was Mr. Victor *"VJ"* Joseph, teacher and disc jockey. I thought he played the best compilations of music for parties around the island. I followed him and his music everywhere. I used that money I had saved to start buying my collection of albums with the plan of being a disc jockey one day, but in the meantime, I just followed *DJ VJ*.

I can clearly remember a common practice we had when on a Sunday night *DJ VJ* played music at a party venue at

Buccoo Point, called *"Sunday School"*. A guy named Paris had made Buccoo Point into a real cool down place for party goers. It became known worldwide so when visitors to our shores arrived here one of the first questions, we got from them was if Sunday School was for adults?

To tell my story; a section of young men from our village who had the same passion as I, would gather at the village recreation club, where all the gamblers were assembled playing cards during the night, and we would borrow their bicycles to make the trip to Buccoo. Because transportation was our biggest problem. And I mean borrow without asking, the thing is we knew who all the bikes' owners were and where they lived. It would be a very short walk home for them after they had their fun, but for us it was a five-mile walk to get home. The bike owners never reported us to the police saying the missing bikes were stolen. So, we knew they understood our plight and sympathized with us. The next morning when they awoke their bikes would be at their gates ready to take them to work as normal.

Anyway, the night in question it was late and we could not see Fatty. He was always late for our adventures at Buccoo. so, that night we borrowed a bike for him, took it to his home and told him we were waiting for him. We did not know how unsettling this would be for him. It made him hurry more than usual as we were all there, it was around five or six of us. He hurried out took the bike got on and we left for Buccoo Point.

Halfway there, hurrying because we didn't want all the nice girls taken before we had our opportunity to make our choices, I noticed him sitting strangely in the saddle.

So, I asked: "What's going on with you Fatty?"

He looked at me like he was really in discomfort and said: "I forgot to put on my underpants, hurrying to not have you all waiting on me."

The others overheard our conversation, and everybody started to laugh at the same time. That night was a disaster for Fatty. He danced with one girl and after that had to leave the hall because his erection exposed his lack of underwear. Along with that everyone had noticed something was wrong when they were dancing, because of the young lady's posture during the dance. She was bent almost halfway forward with her rear end pushed all the way back to avoid touching him. That was the talk of the night and several days after, as a matter of fact. Months passed before Fatty got the courage to venture back to Buccoo Point on another Sunday School night. Just goes to show how some young men have fun while some go through torment. And all of that was courtesy of *DJ VJ*. By the way, he turned ninety-four years old recently. I wish him many more.

He reminded me of the story of the pied piper, people came from near and far to dance to *DJ VJ's* music. And apart from that people would line up waiting for his eight track and cassette recordings to play in their cars and homes. I saw myself following in his footsteps and believe it or not I did follow in his footsteps. I was a DJ and recorded music just like he did with cassettes and compact discs, and I even went on to do music videos on DVDs, taking it a few steps further. So, from being my hero, he was also my mentor. And he was also a native of my village. Thank you, *DJ VJ*. His example of dedication and inspiration is nothing short of heroic and pillar qualifications.

Chapter Thirty-Five

Samuel *"Cojar"* Blacks was first and foremost, a pan man extraordinaire, he slept and woke up with the steelpan on his mind. A total pan man, he loved the steelpan with a passion. I found that out very early in my pan playing life. I realized without having taken music lessons for any instrument like piano or guitar, he just knew his chords for the pan. When he arranged a tune, he did it by ear. By playing the original melody and by branching off the outskirts of the melody, he could find what *phrasing* (*musical phrasing* is the way a musician shapes a sequence of music to allow expression) he desired to sweeten the sound to the ear.

I watched him intently to try and learn from his simple practice, but the man was a genius in himself. That was his style and to learn it would take years off my life and I still would not be able to master it, because that was his and his alone. When I came to that conclusion, I felt a load lifted off my shoulders. There were times when he smoked cigarettes, and I would notice that his concentration on the music was so deep, that the cigarette would burn all the way until the part with the tobacco would fall off leaving just the filter in his mouth, and he would never notice.

Especially if he had to arrange a tune for competition, he was worse. The man became a total wreck and all he needed were his cigarettes one after the other. But he never disappointed. He would put one hundred per cent of himself into the piece of music he was doing. and you could tell by watching his demeanor closely if he appreciated it or not, because he wore his emotions on his proverbial sleeve.

I can clearly remember the days when we played music for the visitors' entertainment at the hotel you could actually feel his joy by his body language. He arranged most, if not all the tunes, so he was in a paradise of his own making and believe me he was a joy to watch. I saw that same joy in him when he played in his church band, yes, he played steelpan in church. *"Cojar"* felt the need to turn his life to Christ and in the Church of the Nazarene he found our Savior. He stopped smoking and gave up the arranging for party music and started arranging music for the church. He even had a small steelpan orchestra playing in the church. *"Cojar"* fell ill and spent some time in hospital, and the orchestra was disbanded when he was hospitalized.

In the hospital things were not going right for him and it got to a stage where the doctors felt there was nothing more, they could do for him, so they discharged him thinking he would just go home and die. God in His wisdom had more for *"Cojar"* to do before taking him home. He got over all his illness as if it was a miracle and he went back to church with his tenor pan of course, playing in accompaniment as he normally would. He had a new lease on life. Samuel Blacks lived a couple more years playing his tenor pan in church with just as much enthusiasm as if he was never sick. For me it was a miracle to witness.

But as it is said, all good things must come to an end sometime, and so it was for Samuel *"Cojar"* Blacks. He was somewhere in his late 80s or early 90s when he passed on, he lived his full life doing just what he was sent here to do without any abbreviations, fear nor favor, he just did it his way.

I am a better person for associating with *"Cojar"*. I know this because he was the captain of the band who invited me to give those double guitars some love at that time. At that stage of my life, I was just drifting, and I think he saw it and felt the need to intervene in a positive way. I must give thanks to Mr. Samuel Blacks for that intervention and guidance. I take my hat off to you sir for all you did in helping to shape my future without even knowing it. He stayed my good friend throughout his life. I miss him and I feel emptiness of not seeing him and his tenor pan at our church. May the good Lord keep blessing him as He spread His wings of love all over Samuel *"Cojar"* Blacks, rest in eternal peace, another pillar of our community.

I am inspired right here, right now, to just say this, *"there are three things that come not back in anyone's life, and they are the spoken word, the spent arrow and a lost opportunity"*. And don't ever think you will be the first to make them happen, especially that last one. Never waste an opportunity you will live to regret it. Also, never let circumstances or any negative attitude impede your way to progress or waste an opportunity to elevate yourself. The onus is always on you to make the right decision, not your parents, nor your best friend, just you, the reason being nobody knows what you need for you better than you, and always believe that you can be the next pillar of your community.

Chapter Thirty-Six

Samuel Harry, son of Joseph *"Big Joe"* Harry, was an unusual personality of my village, not in the way you might think, but give me some time I would try to explain. I knew him as a proud man with thoughts that anything his mind told him to try, he could be great at doing it.

I can start with football; something happened to convince him that he could be good at football. Nothing was further from the reality of the situation, but no one could convince him about the talent he didn't have as far as football playing was concerned. You could know how good an artist is when you give them a plain canvas and ask them to paint something that comes to mind, when they're done you must know if they have talent you could work with or not. He would try very hard to fit in, but where football was concerned, he liked the game, but the game just didn't like him. But I took glory in his spirit and his energy, and I admired him for his output in trying to be good at it. He could kick the ball hard but there was so much more to the game than kicking the ball hard than he knew or realized.

It was a time when we had no coach around to teach or train us as aspiring footballers. But anyone could look at certain aspiring players and see the raw talent they possessed and see there was something there someone could work with. As a matter of fact, I think he played in the soft shoe league.

I am saying all this to highlight where the talent was supposed to go, and where it went eventually. It was in music. The man was a genius pan player and arranger and when he came into his own, he was a joy to behold. I didn't live far from his home where he developed his music capabilities. And while he honed his skills, I was within earshot to enjoy some of his renditions and I would say to myself the proverbial pigeons have finally come home to roost. He had found his element. He had the tenacity to put all he had into his arrangements he came up with for the tunes he picked to work with. And for me they were sweet to my ears, and to top it all off the man never learnt a note of music, everything came by ear. We had a music teacher in one Ms. Gertrude of St Cyr Street, Canaan, who gave piano lessons, and who rode her bicycle to church and everywhere, she lived just opposite Mr. James' bakery, but he felt no need for her professional touch.

His talent, just like *Cojars',* was God given and they were satisfied to exploit their gifts to the fullest. To be able to understand them better you had to listen to them talk about their pan music. To hear the passion with which they expressed their satisfaction for the pieces of music they performed. After a competition, you would think they were Mozart, Bach, Chopin, or even Tchaikovsky, they were so proud. I admired Sam for the way he effortlessly proved himself with his music and without any fanfare, he was regarded as a musicologist and a proud one at that.

Samuel Harry has passed on, but this community will forever remember him for his musical skills and will without any doubt place him in that category as one of the main pillars of our community. May the good Lord bless him and keep him safe under His wings of love forever and ever. I do miss hearing the camaraderie of the two most famous pan professionals of my village. I have a great feeling that as I write this those two guys are already playing their music in those great halls of heaven.

Chapter Thirty-Seven

I had an opportunity to embrace a music idol of mine. One special night, at the back of Reeves Louis' shop, in a real party atmosphere that I will never forget. It was none other than Pal Joey Lewis and his orchestra. Mr. Louis occupied a house at the rear of his shop and having paved that area between shop and residence he made it possible to have meetings there. The talk was that Joey was Reeves' brother, so Reeves said, so entertaining Joey came naturally. I didn't care if he was a brother or not, bring on the music, and along came half of the island to dance to the great Joey Lewis' music. The hall was packed to the brim and overflowed; there were people dancing all in the street.

He played tunes *like "Pint O Wine", "Mother", "Joey's Dance", "Joey's Saga", "Bound to Dance",* and *"You'll Always Be A friend"* to name a few. Just to be able to see Joey play and have the privilege and the pleasure to dance to some of those sounds and watch the maestro at his best on his organ, he played guitar too, was like a dream come true for me. Being young and impressionable, I didn't care that I had no girlfriend, but I was fortunate to have about three what we call sets (to dance with a female partner) that whole night. I didn't care, I was at Pal Joey's Party. My chat the next day to friends was, *"I didn't see you at Joey's party last night",* with a big smile on my face. Showing them what they had missed by just looking at the expression on my face.

That night, to me, was the best reason for Mr. Reeves Louis to be living here at Canaan, other than that he was just another rich shopkeeper. He even took over the bands' bass guitar, (that huge bass was almost as tall as a man, rested on a pivot and looked like an overgrown violin) and proceeded to accompany the band through a disastrous set until the man took back his instrument. And every time you entered his shop after that night you can guess what the topic was.

But as things go, as a businessman, in my opinion, which I am entitled to, I was never impressed by his greedy attitude towards customers. Argumentative and aggressive was the way he came over to me on the one hand. And on the other hand, it seemed like he had an issue with trusting the help he employed. He constantly watched their every move. And when he got to the stage of his life when his children were not around him to take over the everyday running of his shop, he had to oversee every transaction made from beginning to the time the money changed hands and the attendant put his hand in the drawer to make change. I distinctly remembered seeing him on a sofa in the shop. Laying there where he could see everything that went on, even though he was not in any fit state to be up and about.

I could truly say that having experienced some habits of some people, I made up my mind to either follow in their footsteps or not. Mr. Reeves Louis was one of those businessmen who I made a vow very early in life to never follow his style. I saw him as a shop owner who never trusted anyone. If that was the way rich people made all their money, I don't want it.

That was when I came to the realization that I would never want to be rich. I decided then and there, to ask God to make me self-sufficient, that when I need anything, I would be able to afford it and I'll be the happiest man in this world.

I thank God every day for hearing my prayer. I have been blessed each day not having to ask anyone for anything, so if I'm in need no one knows and when I have no one knows. That way no one can say I came begging, cap in hand, for anything. For me it's the best practice in the world. I urge everyone to try it sometime, to me it's a fulfilling lifestyle and if we have more of it, this world will most definitely be a much better place to live in. We learn by experience and association. So, Mr. Reeves Louis, played his part in being a pillar in our community. But his style is not for me.

This building was once Reeves Louis' shop it currently houses a minimart and a mobile phone store.

I am about to delve into another family who came into prominence in more ways than one, they are the Potts family of Bon Accord. They were about culture, as far as drumming was concerned, and were also into goat racing. For the drumming, culturally, I had the opportunity to witness them in action during a festival at Studley Park where my uncle was the main attraction at the time. My uncle's name was Muhtadi, drummer extraordinaire, at least he was. He lived in Canada and played a huge part in the celebration of the Toronto Caribbean Carnival, known to locals as "Caribana." I've had the pleasure of witnessing one over the years, it happens every year around the first week in August.

I must add that you can bet your last dollar with any odds, that it would be the warmest day of the year, and you would smile on your way to the bank. That was how I happened to hear them drumming to their heart's content, and having all who were in attendance tapping their feet or giving a shake to the rhythm. They would also be seen at the goat race meetings with their charges fit and ready to participate and give a good showing of their talent.

Also from humble beginnings, that family now has, I think our second locally grown doctor who was born and bred out of Bon Accord. I could be mistaken, there could be more than two, I will stand corrected if I'm wrong.

Chapter Thirty-Eight

As I mentioned church earlier, I must say that I have a theory about the number of churches in our new town. I'm also of the opinion that no one will be able to make an educated guess as to how many churches we counted in this vicinity of my new town. I'll give you a little time to tax your brain for the number of churches. Just don't ask me to remember all the names because I'll fail that test miserably. There are some names I never heard in my life before, and I've been here awhile, so I just gave up memorizing them.

In the meantime, I will give you my theory about why I think there are so many churches in this area. Brace yourself, in a nutshell what attracts all these worshippers and their ministers to our fair town is nothing but money, the root of all evil. Please don't condemn me for speaking my mind, and because we are talking about churches you might think I should not connect those two dots. Everyone looks to follow the trail of money, so why not ministers. This Is a new thriving community and if you can find everything else, why not churches? Aren't they a part of the fiber of our existence? Yes, of course they are.

The ministers have an option to say that anywhere money circulates there would be souls to be saved, and this is where they should be, So, they are just in their workspace, so can you blame them?

There are over fifteen (15) churches in this new town. I know the oldest one happens to be The Bethesda Gospel Hall Church at Bon Accord, opposite the entrance to Milford Court. That church was built before I was born I can tell because it's the same style as my house, with its short pillar trees, so it has to be over 75 years old. The largest one is the Seventh Day Adventist Church at Guy Street, Canaan, built about four or five years ago.

Above; the oldest church in my village/town Bethesda Gospel Hall

Below the largest church in my town The Seventh Day Adventist Church

One of the newest ones, a little over a year old, is Kingdom Community Fellowship Foundation Church, located at Bon Accord. I was told that there's even a church on the third floor of D Colosseum.

D Colosseum home of the Mahanaim Prophetic Society along with many businesses and government offices

Last, but not least, in Canaan we also care about education in a big way. There is the recently constructed Tobago Technology Center where there are classes for students of Youth Training and Employment Partnership Programme (YTEPP) and MIC Institute of Technology (MIC-IT). At the Center they offer associate degrees and certified courses in a number of areas such as cosmetology, small business, auto and diesel, and welding.

Training Technology Centre home of YTEPP and MIC-IT

Chapter Thirty-Nine

There is one name I would never immediately associate with being a pillar of our community, but I decided to include him for no matter how I look at it, he contributed of sorts. This name is Mr. Lloyd *"Nazi"* George, son of the late Mr. Brandford George. Now to begin to describe this man could take some doing. He was foremost a very good joiner, making cabinets and cupboards. I was told he was very neat in his work, and he took pride in his neatness. He would do a little carpentry too. But the most interesting side of him as far back as I can remember was him erecting a notice board at Canaan.

That notice board was on everybody's lips from one end of Tobago to the next. Cars full of passengers would slow down or stop to read the latest news on it and believe me there was always some type of news put there to read. Whether it was *Nazi* writing up the board we could never tell because he always plead innocence, all he was willing to say was that he was given a job to erect the board and that was all he was responsible for. We all had our suspicions, but no one complained, we were just eager to pass by to see what the latest news was.

And whether most of the news was made up or just hearsay, most times it would put a smile on all the faces reading it. Someone always saw the funny side of what was written there. It might be about someone's husband or wife, but they always left you wondering how they knew these things and in such a quick timing. *Nazi* was something of a comedian because he always saw the funny side of whatever was talked about, and that's the part that won his place here in the pillars of our society.

I can also remember that the last time I witnessed a bongo at a wake at Gaskin, I think, it was Leroy Bristol's grandfathers' wake. It was because *Nazi* was taking part in that bongo, *Flapps* was there also taking part in the bongo. All I can say about the bongo is that it was like a play with different characters beginning with a fellow called Oats and another called Dollar but putting it all together was big fun. If I can recall correctly there was one guy with something with which to beat another if the other said something out of timing, but it was really funny all around, that was Lloyd George. I also think that the Tobago Heritage Festival is all about keeping those long-time traditions alive.

Lloyd migrated to the USA quite a few years ago and from what I heard of him, he had a serious fall and injured his back and must use a wheelchair for mobility. He tried to return home a few years ago but he didn't stay long because his medical needs can only be handled by his doctors in America. But looking on the bright side, he is still alive and kicking and I know if his temperament is the same, he is making someone smile every chance he gets. I ask God to provide to all his needs to keep him well into the future, through the love of His son Jesus Christ.

Chapter Forty

It would be remiss of me not to mention a name that was synonymous with my village. Villain or *"smart man"*? You tell me. Everyone, even the smallest child knew of the late Mr. Joseph *"Carupano"* James. To describe that guy would take some doing, but I would give it my best shot.

I am of the belief that his mother was a lady we all called T. Tazzie, who lived next to T. Coolie, on the corner of Milford Road and George Street at Canaan, just near to where Mr. Reeves Louis had his shop. *Carupano* got that name being one of the men who drifted as a fisherman, to Venezuela and ended up in a village of that same name. Fishing was one of his trades, but I really cannot say if he was any good at it. He was, to me, an opportunist who took on whatever he thought would make a fast dollar.

Having said all of that, hoping to have described him the best way I could, the story that the other fishermen told about the way he got his sobriquet, remains with me until today.

It was said that when they came off the boat at Carupano, after drifting for a few days, they were all accosted by native Venezuelans who were very aggressive toward them as strangers on their shores. The locals called the local police to take care of this new situation. And even though he was not able to speak any Spanish, Mr. Joseph James took up the responsibilities of spokesperson for the group.

While in this capacity he was asked by the officer: *"Como esta usted?"* which in English means, *"How are you?"*

But Mr. James not understanding a word of Spanish blurted out: *"Ahwee nuh come fuh stay, Ahwee ah guh back tomorrow."* In deep Tobago dialect. Meaning: *"We didn't come to stay we are going back tomorrow."*

The statement was very simple but his antics while talking to the officers were too aggressive and they started to beat him and the two other men with him. Everyone got beaten and thrown in jail. Our government had to negotiate their release and send transportation to bring them back here from Carupano. That was how he got that name *"Carupano"* which stuck on him until the day he died.

That was the caliber of the man, pushy and arrogant and always thinking he was smarter than everyone else. I also have another story about him in my first book, *("The Shadow of Fear and Hunger").* He even got caught stealing another man's fish pot out at sea and the owner of the fish pot relieved him of his right hand at the wrist and was jailed for two years for the incident. The worst part of it was to see him fighting to light his cigarette with one hand, almost losing half of the box of matches. And because of his reputation nobody would help him, thinking he fully deserved losing his hand. If you stole a man's fish pot you stole his livelihood, and his ability to make ends meet for his whole family. May he finally rest in peace.

To a more pleasant topic now. We were blessed with members of our village with qualifications to enable them to serve on seats in our Tobago House of Assembly (THA). Starting with my good friend and football teammate, the late Mr. George "Cacho" Archer, who served two terms and brightened up our recreation ground with lights for activities at night, so we could have basketball, netball and football under the lights. He passed on a couple of years ago to everyone's dismay. He went to the hospital for a ruptured appendix, what everybody thought would have been routine surgery, next thing the family was preparing for his funeral, it was one of the most unwarranted preparations. Everyone was caught up in the same state of mind asking the same questions, we understand in the midst of life we are all in death, but this case left the same bad taste in everyone's mouth.

We were classmates from elementary school, and he excelled in his lessons. He graduated to trade school in Trinidad and when he returned to Tobago he was employed at the Trinidad and Tobago Electricity Commission at Scarborough. He was an avid footballer, we played on the Somerset team of the early 1970s. He had the sweetest left foot shot you could ask for and was my left half, what we call an attacking left side midfielder today. He played alongside Rupert Franklyn, they were like the dynamic duo of Batman and Robin, please don't ask who would take the mantle of Batman, that would cause a big argument. I always felt much better knowing that those two guys had my back, being the striker I was, I could always depend on both of them and most of the goals I scored had assist by either one of them written all over them, Leroy Bristol chipped in now and then from my right wing.

George was so cool, calm, and collected that when during his early retirement, he spent his time doing the trade he loved, that's welding. He was chosen to campaign for the vacant seat on The House of Assembly at the upcoming elections, we all knew he was just a shoe in or a sure thing. He won his first term in office and took his post very seriously. As an Assemblyman he was a success because he was voted back in office for a second four-year term.

I consider him to be one of the stalwarts who left us too soon, but God in His wisdom was in control then as He is now, so who am I to question His actions. My wish is for George to be sheltered under the wings of love that God provides for His children whom He thinks have done their job well. I could always say one thing about my good friend, he was such a gentleman throughout his life, I never heard him say a bad word or get upset to argue or curse, not once.

Then there was the late Mr. Lennox *"Joylie"* Smith, the late Mr. Frank Roberts, Mr. Huey Cadette, Mr. Rolly Quaccoo and Mr. Clarence Jacob, who served one term each. This entire community was blessed by our Master Himself. By sending all of these differently qualified individuals to maintain this special standard that our village could depend on to help it move forward to where it is today.

This community is now so well equipped to take care of all our needs in every department anyone can think of that we bow to those who went before us paving the way for us in every avenue necessary to facilitate every facet of society.

The village has captivated not only the First Citizens Bank to move its biggest bank to Canaan but a whole section of businesses have migrated and are still migrating from the capital of Scarborough to our new town. So, we are now the most capable village/town in Tobago, where services are concerned.

We are here to cater from foundation to fixtures, from medicinal supplies, to buying a new car or truck, from household necessities, to restaurants, and from reef tours to flying out to London and beyond. Touching every avenue of this modern technological age, we are ready.

Chapter Forty-One

I will not forgive myself if I didn't mention two pillars at this juncture of my story, one has passed on, may his soul rest in peace, and the other is still here with us, Thank God, for Mr. Selwyn *"Teepoo"* Archer. The first pillar of this chapter's name was the late Mr. Johnathan *"Bat"* Thomas, he was given that nickname because of his prowess with a cricket bat. It was very difficult to get him out of his wicket on any good day, he would bat all day, and he was a joy to behold in that wicket, but he never bragged about his talent. He was one of the two guys who helped feed me to have some strength to play football. I had a little talent there and they saw my potential and volunteered to help me, seeing my need, for which I am eternally grateful.

"Bat" worked at the Breakfast Shed, right next to the Fire Station Headquarters at Bacolet Street, Scarborough, where some organization took it upon themselves to feed the poor and needy around the town area, people just like me, but in my case living at Canaan. I had to find my way to Scarborough to get my lunch or I would not eat. It was an adventure for me on the days when I had to go to town, on those days when Selwyn was not available to help. You might wonder why I needed the help from those guys. It was after the coup of 1970, and I had returned to Tobago and started playing football with Somerset and all I had was my truck driver's license and driving jobs were not popular there were not many trucks around like there are now.

Anyway, without a doubt I relished the adventure when I had to get to town, knowing the reward was getting my belly full so I never got frustrated, except if I didn't get there in time to help *"Bat"* clean up. That was a part of our agreement that I must come in time to help him clean up, but sometimes no matter how I tried I would still get there late. On those occasions *"Bat"* would just shake his head with a little smile and show me where to get my food. It didn't happen often though, because some of the taxi drivers had seen me play and loved my style, so seeing me on the road walking they would stop and give me a ride just to talk about a game they saw me playing in, or maybe about a goal I had scored.

Coming home was much easier because Bat always had bus tickets. He was a gem of a man, no doubt about that. He is sorely missed, and I know because of his big heart he is being well taken care of sheltered as he surely is under wings of love by our God and Savior of us all. Hence another pillar, for his wonderful humility and the presence of mind to assist without even being asked. I thank God for men like him every day.

The other big-hearted man I must mention here is Mr. Selwyn *"Teepoo"* Archer, and I'm proud to reveal that he was the *"Cassa"* who made sure that a certain young man got all he desired to make football trials in Trinidad. If it was not for *"Teepoo"*, that young man would not have had that career. And I'm not just saying that because I could, It's the gospel truth. *"Teepoo"* can also be credited for hiding his mother's food so I would have something to eat to keep up my strength to play football.

I do believe in honesty and what goes around, comes around. Also, I must give credit where credit is due, because every man, woman, or child must pay for their actions. No one can expect to plant corn and reap peas, always expect that what you sow that is what you will reap, come what may. My father used to say, God never wears pajamas, so He sees everything and pays all debts without money, according to how they work. In other words, He is qualified as the best accountant in the universe, nothing gets by Him.

And having said all of that, I must say that my hat goes off to my friend Mr. Selwyn Archer, who is still very much alive and well today. I do wish him a very long life to keep on doing those good things he has been doing. To make it nicer, he comes from a father, Mr. Daniel *"Slow Joe"* Archer, an export worker, and husband to our greatest teacher, the late teacher *"Baby Joe"*. Another pillar in our community along with his son.

Last but not least, we must celebrate all the centurions; those who have passed on, and the still living 101-year-old Mr. Daniel *"Slow Joe"* Archer, the husband of the late Mrs. Annetta *"Baby Joe"* Archer, who recently passed away at 90 something years old.

I must say congratulations to *"Slow Joe"* for his contribution towards making our entire community the lovely place it is today. And I do wish him many, many more birthdays, and that God will continue to shower him with blessings in abundance. I just realized it was *Baby Joe* and *Slow Joe,* what a thing!

Among those whom have passed on the oldest of them was the late Mrs. Martha Waldron Thomas, born July 19, 1919, and passed away on August 23, 2023. She was 104 years old, such a gentle lady, always selling and sharing her fruits by the side of the road. Mrs. Martha was the mother of four boys, who along with her husband, Mr. Bobsy Thomas, all died before her, they were Ardill, Justin, John and Pernell Thomas. May she rest in peace, sheltered under His wings of love.

There was also the late Mr. Knolly Henry, father of Harrigan, Bertill and Bernard "Sprat" Henry, he was also 104 years old. May he rest in peace sheltered under His wings of eternal love.

There was Mr. Roderick "Roddy" Boyce, he gave us 102 years of his time. He was another pioneer who told us how he worked at the Bon Accord estate for $0.15 cents a day picking up coconuts to throw into the tractors' trailer to take into the yard for cutting open to be dried to make copra. May he rest in Peace sheltered under His wings of love.

Chapter Forty-Two

Having come to almost the end of my stroll down memory lane you can clearly see from my recollections the direction in which you were taken. And I am positive you were not bored or dissatisfied with most, if not all the pillars and stories of the interesting people, who graced my village and helped to make it what it has become today. I would like to think that there are many more stories, and pillars, still around in all the other villages on our little island waiting to be told.

I'm not sure if I can remember every one of those pioneers, but I challenge others to continue where I left off so nothing goes under the carpet. I send out a challenge right here, right now. Let what was read here motivate or inspire at least one person to commit some of their time to resurrect some of their stories. If not for the pleasure of the memories, like myself, then do it for the youths of today. Give them something to ponder. After all, we always hear the talk about they don't have any boy/girl days growing up in a technological era. They never *"spin a top, fly a kite, make a crab trap, pitch marbles or run a pony race".* What they know is Tik Tok, WhatsApp, Instagram, Netflix and YouTube. Family time now is cheap. Parents have nothing to spend quality time doing with their children, as far as teaching them something worthwhile is concerned.

If the maestro himself, Mr. Winston Bailey (The Mighty Shadow) could make a big hit by bringing back the devil Abyssinia in calypso, and as the youths of today would say, bigging him up along with Mt. Thomas, the village in which he lived, we can bring back our village heroes.

I'm in my 70s and I can distinctly remember running from Abyssinia as a boy, when all he did was open his mouth at me. He had no teeth, but just his body movements as a painted black devil with that fork in his hand on carnival day, would make anybody run. Even other playing devils were scared of him. And the Mighty Shadow had the whole country jumping, singing about him. Just use your imagination, you don't have to be another Shadow to make a difference. We all have a story to tell, because we all have different experiences and believe me when I say, that when stories are told there is someone somewhere who benefits wholeheartedly from another's experience.

Almost every Saturday morning I hear Mr. Al Joe saying on the radio, that by calypsos our stories are told. I refute that statement here and now, to be only partly true, because I am a perfect example by writing all those stories in these my three books now. Sorry Al Joe, I had to contradict you here, no harm, no foul. It is true that we are in a different time, some things have changed, but as people, we are the same, we live, love and laugh out loud the same. And with a little adjustment we just fall into place and go with the flow. I hope that I was able to bring some of the joy to you that I had writing all those stories of my ancestors and acquaintances, that we can all look forward to having more time together to express ourselves another time.

I am so entrenched in inspiring others that every day I keep looking for uplifting stories to write in the hope that once my stories are read someone can be inspired to the point where they would endeavor to call a friend and relate the story hoping that it would have the desired effect on them too.

In my summary of the pillars, I must be cognitive of the fact that most of the ancestors of this village were heroes within their own right. having to succeed in anything those days was like pushing a car up a steep hill. There were no streetlights, no electricity, and that would mean shorter days because as soon as it got dark all work stopped. Hence things would take twice as long to complete. Also, there were no big banks like there are now to loan money to these young entrepreneurs. Money had to be taken from family wealth, hence a much bigger risk. But they did it and we are the ones who stand to benefit from all their sacrifices.

To show all my appreciation and gratitude is why I came up with this idea to do this project by trying to keep their hopes up for a better tomorrow. And as a source of inspiration too, if someone reads these stories and feels it worthwhile to jump on the bandwagon, feel free to do one too. We all have a story tell and I promise you there will always be somebody somewhere to read or listen to your story. And who knows, by reading this book one day someone may come up to a name and say: "that was my grandfather", nothing would please me more than for that to happen. Because I'm sure it would be said with much pride and humility and that was one of my reasons for this book.

The other reason was to pay homage to all those who did their thing their way and had to leave when they were called home. We are here doing our thing our way because of what they started, for example the house I'm living in right now is the same house where I was born over seven decades ago and it's only recently, I had one leak. They really knew how to build long ago and I'm showing my deep appreciation for what I call old school construction. There was no time for shortcuts, they did it the right way or not at all.

I did some renovation over the years, but I really am a true old school child, I love the way my home and I fit together. I can walk through it with my eyes closed and find everything I need, that's why I told my children there will be no home for the aged for me. I can look at a corner of my home and all the memories come flooding back, I love that. I can still remember what hurricane Flora soaked down and what it broke, like it was yesterday.

I drive around my community now and notice all the changes with total admiration and appreciation. I have tried many times to try fitting myself in some of those ancestors' shoes and I can feel my toes being squeezed for a proper fit. My mind even went back to my days with a shoehorn, yeah I had one, but the comfortable fit would not come because those guys were cut from a different bolt of cloth than us. They were born heroes, so whatever they touched just turned to gold. In closing this chapter, I would like to give kudos to each one of the pillars mentioned and I hope that I have given everyone else some food for thought.

I do feel a sense of pride, gratitude and inspiration for all of those, past and present, who with their selfless contributions made all of this possible so that I can project more goodwill to all the world. Also, in the hope that others can follow in the footsteps I left here by opening the door for them to collaborate with themselves to show others what their villages can offer to visitors and also to give the youths something to hold on to beside crime and dishonesty.

We are already handicapped by Trinidad, having to do without some basic amenities. So, let's just try and make it easier and more accessible for the younger ones to adapt to a better lifestyle by learning about our heroes who had much less than what we do have now, but never complained and still made a good life for us and helped us to be where we are today. And I reiterate, this is a practice that anyone can initiate, our villages brought us up so it takes nothing special to follow in my footsteps.

All you have to do is tell yourself you are not doing it for you but for the whole new generation coming behind. Give them an insight into their past. Your story is there waiting to be told but if you never tell it, you deprive the world of something unique. Everyone has their own story, and you might be surprised the reception you might get on coming out of your proverbial closet. May God bless all my readers and shower them with love eternal.

References

Bobb, Lincoln. Interview via WhatsApp, 5th December 2023.

Franklyn, Rupert "Rupee". Interviewed at his residence at Canaan, Tobago. 20th November 2023.

https://www.aspiringmindstandt.com/russel-mar

https://www.ibtimes.com/buccoo-goat-and-crab-race-festival-tobago-island-enthralls-tourists-photos-555046#slideshow/115888 Photo credit: REUTERS/Andrea De Silva

https://images.app.goo.gl/7Lpo1ZQP33DenZeM8.Goat Racing at Buccoo. Tobago House of Assembly

https://tntairports.com/NEW/history.html

Melville, Jaiye. Interview via WhatsApp 7th December, 2023.

Percy, Lucille. Interview via WhatsApp, 5th December 2023.

Roberts, Rebecca. Interview via WhatsApp, 5th December 2023.

Sandy, Bevon, interviewed at his residence at Signal Hill, Tobago. 25th November 2023.

Skeete, Winston "Man Baby" interviewed at my residence at Canaan, Tobago. 6th December 2023.

Williams, Linton. Interview via WhatsApp, 5th December 2023.

About The Author

Ken G. Gordon is a native of Trinidad and Tobago. He was born in 1947 on the island of Tobago. He is extremely proud of his Tobagonian heritage which is the driving force behind the authorship of his book the Pillars of My Town. Mr. Gordon is also the author of two other works.; The Shadow of Fear and Hunger and Men Have Feelings Too!

By his own declaration he seeks to motivate and inspire through his honest and forthright literary works.

Made in the USA
Columbia, SC
09 January 2025